Highlights

brainPLAY
TRICKIEST PUZZLES EVER

BOOKS FOR PUZZLE PEOPLE

Kid tested by
Veda Kork
Age 11

HIGHLIGHTS PRESS
Honesdale, Pennsylvania

TEST YOUR EYESIGHT

WHAT IS THIS?

HINT: I'm showing my true colors. (But they may change!)

BE LOGICAL

Farmer Ann has 15 cows. Today, all but 9 of them are grazing in the field. The rest are in the barn. How many of Farmer Ann's cows are in the barn?

NOTICE THE DETAILS

What do the robots in each row (vertically, horizontally, and diagonally) have in common?

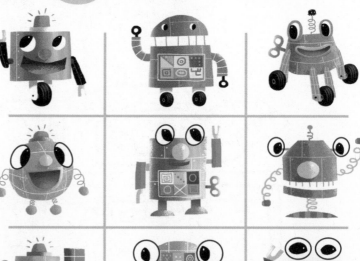

STRETCH YOUR MATH SKILLS

This is one two-rrific math problem! Use the signs for addition (+), subtraction (−), multiplication (×), or division (÷) between the 2s to come up with the answer at the end of each row.

$$(2 \quad 2) \, 2 \quad 2 \quad 2 = 0$$
$$(2 \quad 2 \quad 2) \, 2 \quad 2 = 1$$
$$2 \quad 2 \quad 2 \quad 2 \quad 2 = 2$$
$$2 \quad 2 \quad 2 \quad 2 \quad 2 = 3$$
$$(2 \quad 2) \, 2 \quad 2 \quad 2 = 4$$
$$(2 \quad 2 \quad 2) \, 2 \quad 2 = 5$$

HINT: Here's one way to solve the first equation:
$$(2 - 2) \times 2 \times 2 \times 2 \times 2 = 0$$

TICKLE YOUR FUNNY BONE

When do astronauts eat lunch?

At launch time.

DO A WORD WORKOUT

Use the clues to name words that begin or end with **OR**.

Fruit with a peel

Writer of a book

You walk on it

It helps power a car

A type of whale

Your heart is one

LET'S SHIFT GEARS

START

Make your way from START to FINISH. Then find the mouse, binoculars, top hat, boot, key, butterfly, candle, and Earth.

FINISH

Tulip Time

Find the impostor in this group of tulips. It holds hot liquids and has a handle. Can you also find 12 bees?

DEEP-SEA DINER

FIND THESE OBJECTS IN THE SCENE.

artist's brush
banana
bell
broom
cane

envelope
eyeglasses
fishhook
flashlight
golf club

hat
heart
hockey stick
magnet
needle

paper clip
piece of popcorn
ring
ruler
sailboat

shoe
snake
sock
tack
traffic light

Balloon Animal sudoku

Every balloon animal should only appear once in each row, column, and 2 × 3 box. Fill in the squares by writing down the color or number of each balloon animal.

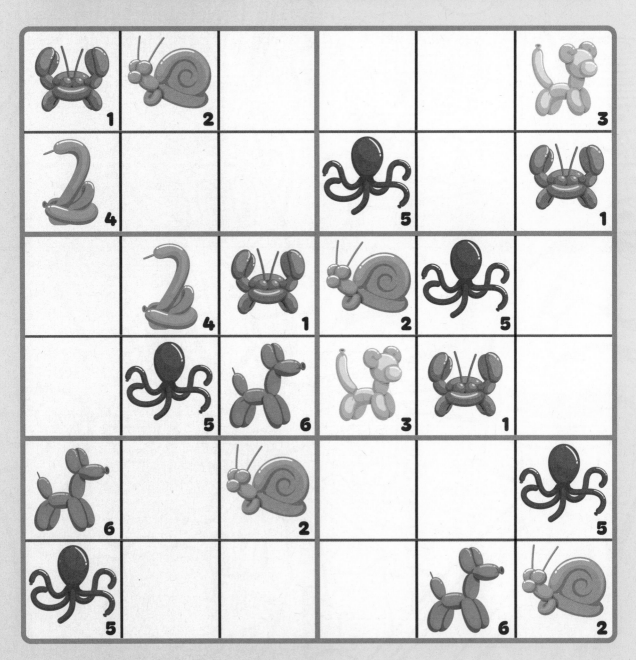

Thumbs up

Each thumbprint has an exact match. Can you find all 12 pairs?

DO THE ROBOT!

Without clues or knowing what to look for, can you find the 24 hidden objects at the Robo Disco party?

What's a robot's favorite music?

Heavy metal.

Puzzling PUPS

Amanda, Noah, and Jamie are picking up their dogs from Top-Dog Training School. Using the clues below, can you match each dog with its age, its owner, and the trick it knows best?

	Wiggles	Rocket	Pawla
Two years old			
Three years old			
Four years old			
Amanda			
Noah			
Jamie			
"Heel"			
"Sit"			
"Come"			

Use the chart to keep track of your answers. Put an **X** in each box that can't be true and an **O** in boxes that match.

CLUES

1 The oldest dog, Pawla, has learned to "heel" but still needs to work on "sit" and "come."

2 Noah's three-year-old dog is one year younger than Amanda's and one year older than Jamie's.

3 Wiggles always comes when called.

4 Rocket is two years old.

60-second stumper

Unscramble the letters below to answer the riddle.

I B K T R C E T A

What do you call a dog that designs doghouses?

A _ _ _ _ _ _ _ – _ _ _ _ _ _ _ _.

check it out

Figure out where these 10 pieces go in the puzzle.

WHERE'S THE CAT?

Cats may have 9 lives, but they also have 26 words in this puzzle. Circle the words containing CAT hidden in the grid. The word CAT has been replaced with a 🐱. Look up, down, across, backward, and diagonally. The uncircled letters answer the trivia question.

WORD LIST

BOBCAT
CATALOG
CATAMARAN
CATBIRD
CATCHY
CATEGORY
CATERPILLAR
CATFISH
CATHEDRAL

CATNAP
CATNIP
CATTAIL
CATTLE
CATWALK
COMMUNICATE
COPYCAT
DECATHLON
DEDICATE

DOGCATCHER
EDUCATION
LOCATE
MULTIPLICATION
SCATTERED
TOMCAT
VACATION
WILDCAT

TRIVIA QUESTION!
what taste are cats unable to detect?
Put the uncircled letters in order from left to right, starting at the top row.

ANSWER: _ _ _ _ _ _ _ _ _'_ _ _ _ _ _ _ _

_ _ _ _ _ _ _ _ _ _ _ .

D O G  C H E R C A ☐ M Y

D T D D W T O M ☐ D T U H

E E C E R A S D C E A L C

☐ ☐ R O D I L A ☐ R I T ☐

H O A N M I B K Y E L I N

L L L A W M ☐ ☐ P T T P E

O T L R A P U E O ☐ S L E

N ☐ I A ☐ T A N C S T I D

E F P M E S ☐ N I ☐ W ☐ U

P I R A G B E E ☐ ☐ T I ☐

I S E ☐ O ☐ A L O G E O I

N H ☐ B R N V A ☐ I O N O

☐ E S S Y L A R D E H ☐ N

LOTS OF LAUNDRY

It's the perfect day to hang laundry out to dry! Can you find the 25 objects hidden in this scene? Can you also find 9 pairs of matching socks?

OBJECTS TO FIND

artist's brush, banana, bat, eyeglasses, bunch of grapes, flag, horseshoe, hourglass, ice-cream cone, kite, ladybug, open book, orange, pear, pencil, present, rake, ruler, sailboat, slice of watermelon, snake, stopwatch, tennis ball, tent, toothbrush

lounging llamas

Find one trio of nearly identical llamas, four pairs of nearly identical llamas, and one llama with no match.

60-second stumper

Say this tongue twister five times, fast: **Mama Llama's pajama drama.**

BEACH DAY

Compare these two beach pictures. Can you find at least 20 differences?

sweet treat patterns

Find each pattern below in the grid.

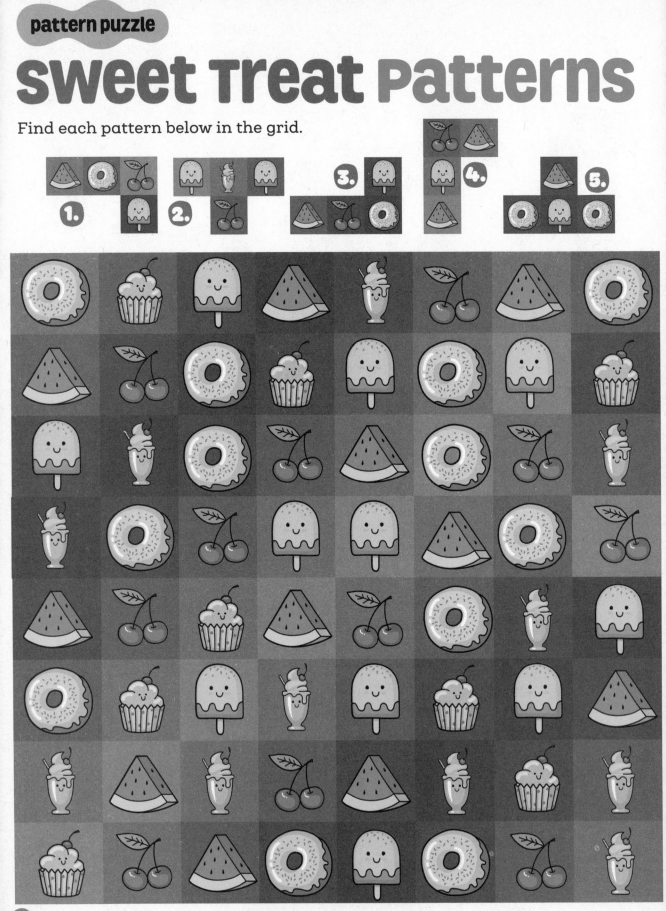

SNOWY VILLAGE

Find your way from START to FINISH. Then find 3 hearts in the scene.

maze

START

FINISH

21

DINO MUSIC FEST

Rock on, dinos! Can you find a beach ball, a hot dog, a striped hat, 4 pairs of twin dinos, a backpack, a red flag, an ice-cream cone, a green T-shirt, 3 baseball caps, a watermelon, and a pink chair?

CONES

DINO-PALOOZA

SECURITY

creepy crawly quizzy

Read each sentence below and circle **T** if you think it's true and **F** if you think it's false.

T F **1.** Insects have been around for more than 400 million years, even before the dinosaurs.

T F **2.** Three types of dragonfly can breathe fire.

T F **3.** All ladybugs are female.

T F **4.** Even other insects think that cockroaches are gross.

T F **5.** In warmer weather, crickets chirp faster.

T F **6.** It takes one year for a centipede to cross all of its legs.

T F **7.** Houseflies live for only one month.

T F **8.** Some swarms of cicadas are as loud as a rock concert.

T F **9.** Stinkbugs can only hang out together if they wear nose plugs.

T F **10.** The praying mantis is the only insect that can turn its head.

T F **11.** Spiders have eight legs, which means they're not insects.

T F **12.** Bees are one of the only insects that produce food that humans eat—honey.

BE LOGICAL

Which pineapple should go in place of each question mark so that each column and row contains all four pineapples?

STRETCH YOUR MATH SKILLS

Place the numbers 1 through 9 in the circles so that each line of three adds up to 15.

TICKLE YOUR FUNNY BONE

HA HA !!

Why didn't the dog go swimming at the beach?

The waves were too ruff.

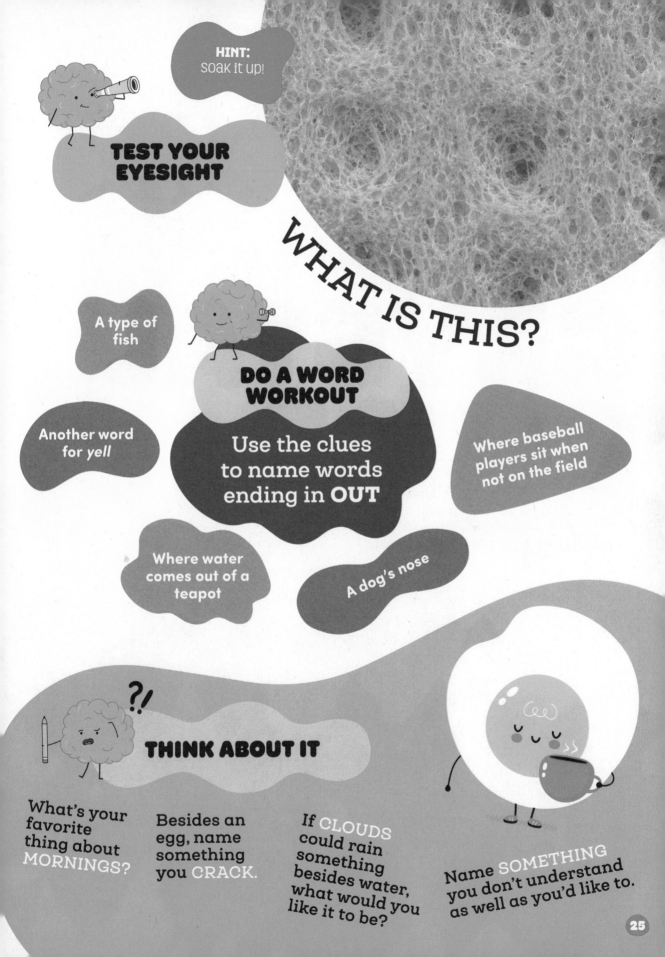

HINT: soak it up!

TEST YOUR EYESIGHT

WHAT IS THIS?

DO A WORD WORKOUT

Use the clues to name words ending in **OUT**

A type of fish

Another word for *yell*

Where baseball players sit when not on the field

Where water comes out of a teapot

A dog's nose

THINK ABOUT IT

What's your favorite thing about MORNINGS?

Besides an egg, name something you CRACK.

If CLOUDS could rain something besides water, what would you like it to be?

Name SOMETHING you don't understand as well as you'd like to.

CRYSTAL CLEAR

Can you find the 20 cotton swabs in this photo of amethyst crystals?

ESCAPE THE CAVE

You're walking along the beach when you stumble upon a cave entrance. You've heard stories about a mysterious millionaire who is said to have hidden her treasure somewhere in these caves long ago. Why not take a look? As soon as you enter, a stone rolls over the opening. You're trapped! Torches burst into flame, lighting up the cave. You notice a letter.

You'll never find my treasure, and you'll be trapped here forever! I've created a maze that only someone as clever as me can solve. To escape, you'll have to choose the path with the correct answer to each clue. But be careful. Wrong pathways will lead to dangerous dead ends.

START

6

9

A man has 15 seashells. He loses all but 9 of them. How many seashells does he have left?

B

A

Coral is Sandy's son's aunt's daughter's sister. What is the relationship between Coral and Sandy?
A. Coral is Sandy's cousin.
B. Coral is Sandy's niece.

What number does the crab represent?

$1 + 4 =$ 🐚

🐚 $-$ 🦀 $= 2$

3

4

If you folded this shape into a cube with the letter *B* on top, which letter would be on the bottom?

A B F
E B C D

A

D

Mr. and Mrs. Dune have five daughters. Each daughter has one brother. How many people total are in the Dune family?

8   12

One of these three paths will lead to the treasure and your freedom. Start at the 5 in the top left corner. Move to a new square by adding 5 or subtracting 3. Move up, down, left, or right. The correct path will lead you to a way out.

This chamber has squares on the floor with numbers written on them. The note says:

5	10	17	10
5	7	12	13
11	6	9	8
16	19	7	11

FINISH

29

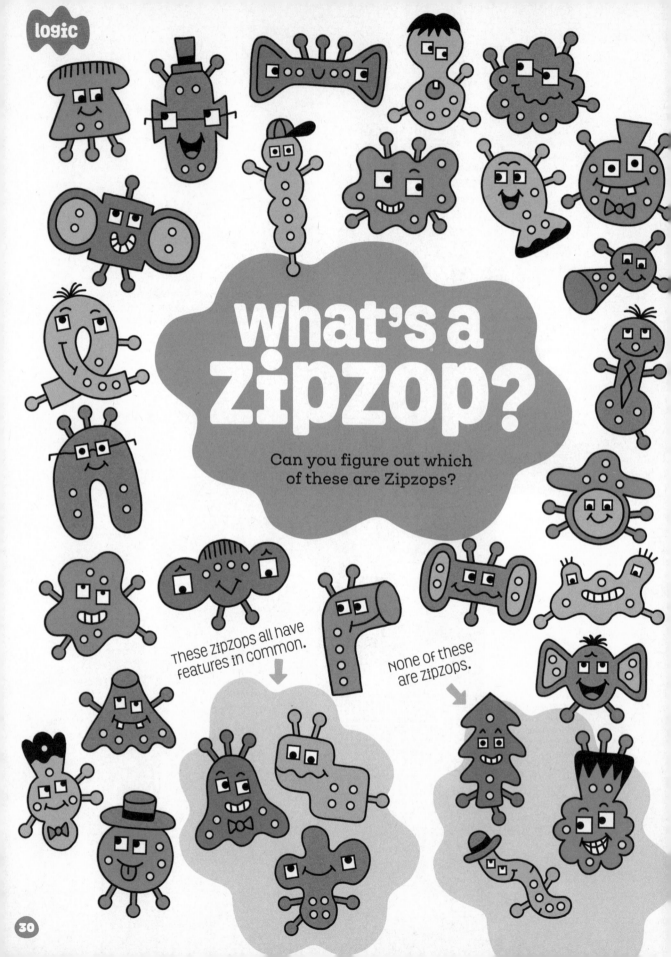

what's a zipzop?

Can you figure out which of these are Zipzops?

These zipzops all have features in common.

None of these are zipzops.

30

seashell shadow match

Take a look at the shadows and match each one to the correct shell below.

A.
B.
C.
D.
E.
F.
G.
H.
I.
J.

There's a lot going on at the Dough-licous Delights bakery today! At least nine objects or actions in this sweet scene rhyme with the word *dough*. Can you find them all?

sea star search

Find the impostor in this group of sea stars. It can change color and has long limbs. Can you also find 12 seashells?

SLOTH RACE

ice-cream cone

pencil

eyeglasses

bell

crescent moon

spoon

fish

banana

drinking straw

ruler

bowl

crown

envelope

fishhook

golf club

needle

LOCK **mess**

Can you figure out which key fits into each lock?

monster sudoku

Every monster should only appear once in each row, column, and 2 × 3 box. Fill in the squares by writing down the color or number of each monster.

What do monsters put on their sundaes?

Whipped scream.

SNOW DAY!

Without clues or knowing what to look for, can you find the 29 hidden objects buried in this snowy scene?

ICE-CREAM CHALLENGE

America's top 10 favorite ice-cream flavors are listed here. Can you crack the code and fill in their names? Each number stands for a different letter. Once you know one number's letter, you can fill in that letter in all the words.

We'll give you a hint—vanilla and chocolate take the first two spots!

60-second stumper

How many gallons of milk does it take to produce 1 gallon of ice cream?

A. 8 gallons   B. 5 gallons   C. 3 gallons

1. ___ ___ ___ ___ ___ ___ ___
   3 2 7 12 10 10 2

2. ___ ___ ___ ___ ___ ___ ___ ___
   8 1 11 8 11 10 2 19 6

3. ___ ___ ___ ___ ___ ___ ___
   8 11 11 17 12 6 18

   ___ ___ ___   ___ ___ ___ ___ ___
   2 7 13   8 4 6 2 14

4. ___ ___ ___ ___
   14 12 7 19

   ___ ___ ___ ___ ___ ___ ___ ___
   8 1 11 8 11 10 2 19 6

   ___ ___ ___ ___
   8 1 12 9

5. ___ ___ ___ ___ ___ ___ ___ ___
   8 1 11 8 11 10 2 19 6

   ___ ___ ___ ___   ___ ___ ___ ___ ___ ___
   8 1 12 9   8 11 11 17 12 6

   ___ ___ ___ ___ ___
   13 11 20 22 1

6. ___ ___ ___ ___ ___ ___   ___ ___ ___ ___ ___
   5 20 19 19 6 4   9 6 8 2 7

7. ___ ___ ___ ___ ___ ___   ___ ___ ___ ___ ___
   8 11 11 17 12 6   13 11 20 22 1

8. ___ ___ ___ ___ ___ ___ ___ ___ ___ ___
   18 19 4 2 16 5 6 4 4 15

This flavor is made up of #1, #2, and #8!

9. ___ ___ ___ ___ ___   ___ ___ ___ ___ ___ ___
   14 11 11 18 6   19 4 2 8 17 18

10. ___ ___ ___ ___ ___ ___ ___ ___ ___ ___
    7 6 2 9 11 10 12 19 2 7

The average American eats more than **23 pounds** of ice cream per year.

have a seat

There are 12 students in this class: Aiden, Brian, Carlos, Dave, Eric, Frank, Grace, Haley, Iris, Jada, Katie, and Lily. Use the clues below to figure out which seat belongs to which kid.

1. Dave sits in the seat farthest from the clock.

2. Brian sits between Lily and Katie and in front of Haley.

3. Eric sits between Haley and Jada, in front of Iris, and behind Lily.

4. Jada sits in front of Frank and behind Dave.

5. Grace sits in a corner behind Carlos.

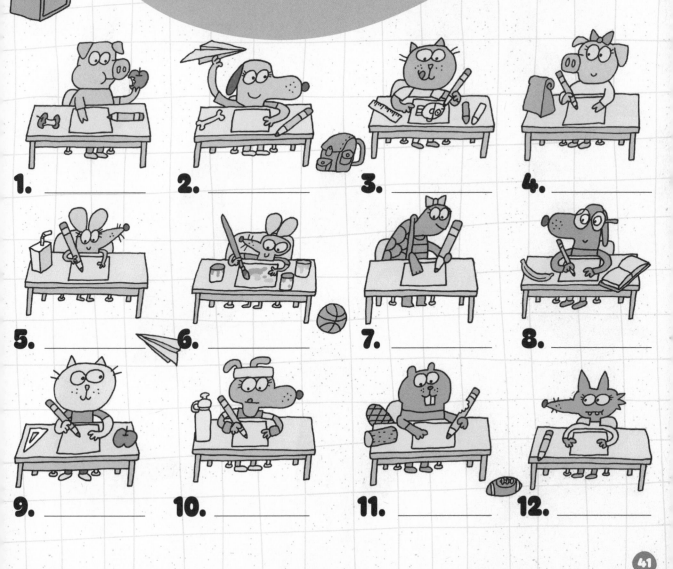

1. _____

2. _____

3. _____

4. _____

5. _____

6. _____

7. _____

8. _____

9. _____

10. _____

11. _____

12. _____

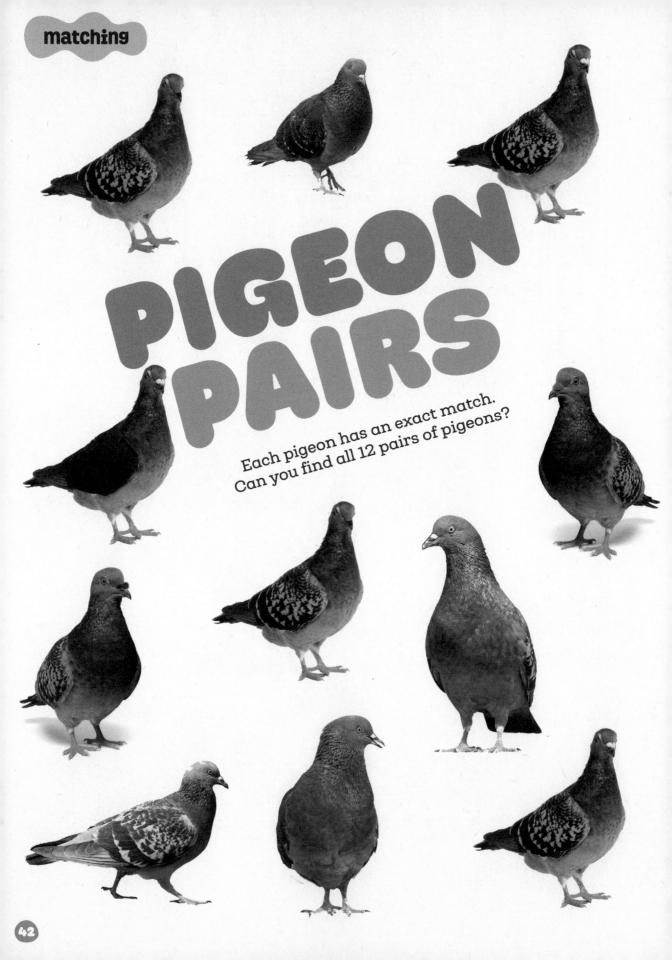

PIGEON PAIRS

Each pigeon has an exact match.
Can you find all 12 pairs of pigeons?

TRAFFIC CHECK

The traffic on the left side of this highway is almost exactly the same as the traffic on the right. But there are a few differences. Can you find 12 differences between the two sides of the highway?

60-second stumper: How many words can you make using the letters in the words *ROAD TRIP*?

DOG DaYS

Figure out where these 8 pieces go in the puzzle.

BE LOGICAL

There is a row of six glasses on the table. The first three glasses are full of orange juice, and the next three are empty. By picking up only one glass, how can you make the empty and full glasses alternate?

DO A WORD WORKOUT

For each pair, think of a word that fits both at the end of the first word and the start of the second word. You'll have two new words!

CAT_ _ _KIN

LIGHT_ _ _ _ _KEEPER

HORSE_ _ _ _YARD

STAR_ _ _ _NET

SNOW_ _ _KIND

SLEEP_ _ _ _BOARD

Example:
MOUNTAIN S I D E WALK
(MOUNTAINSIDE and SIDEWALK)

STRETCH YOUR MATH SKILLS

The numbers in each set of flowers follow a pattern. Find the patterns and figure out which numbers are missing!

A.

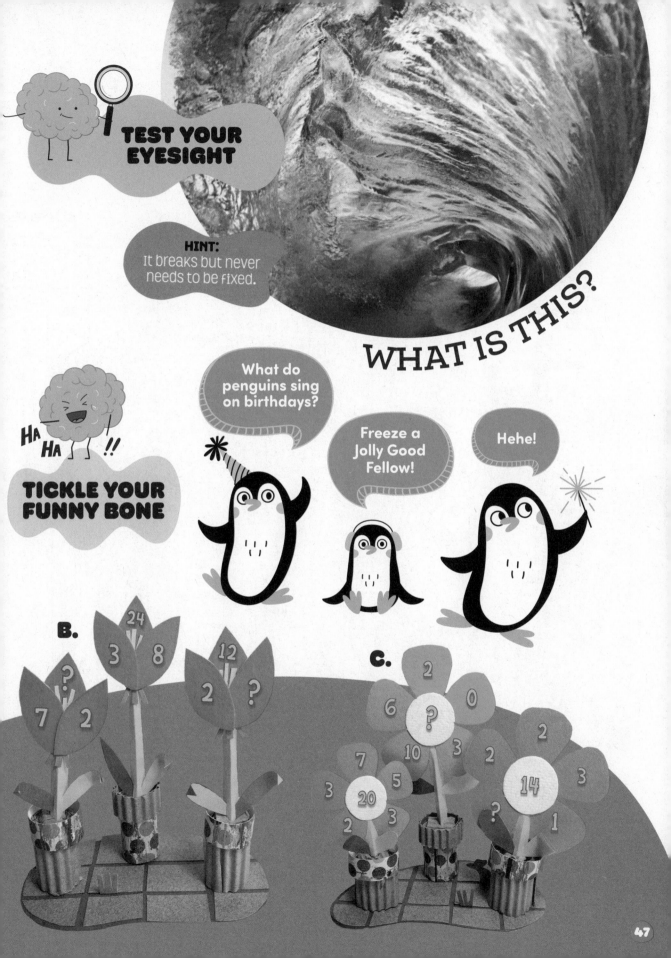

TEST YOUR EYESIGHT

HINT: It breaks but never needs to be fixed.

WHAT IS THIS?

TICKLE YOUR FUNNY BONE

HA HA !!

What do penguins sing on birthdays?

Freeze a Jolly Good Fellow!

Hehe!

B.

24
3 8
?
12
7 2
2 ?

C.

2
6 ? 0
2
10 3
7
3 5 2
20 ?
2 3
14 3
? 1

47

welcome to Sillyville

Wacky things happen all the time in the town of Sillyville. In all this goofiness, can you find a duck, a green umbrella with blue polka dots, a cat, 2 dogs, a pair of star-patterned rain boots, a rainbow, and 4 objects that rhyme with the word *rain*?

Find 9 blue letters in the scene and unscramble them to answer this riddle:

Why is it better to eat doughnuts in the rain? Because you get more

_____.

Tic Tac Cake

What do the cakes in each row
(horizontally, vertically, and diagonally)
have in common?

rink THINK

Four friends are going roller-skating at the local roller rink. Each arrives at a different time, and each gets a different treat from the snack bar. Can you use the clues to figure out each friend's arrival time and snack?

	1:00	1:15	1:30	1:45	hot cocoa	ice cream	hot dog	soft pretzel
Hugo								
Nora								
Gunnar								
Ursula								

Use the chart to keep track of your answers. Put an **X** in each box that can't be true and an **O** in boxes that match.

CLUES

1 Hugo arrived before Nora but after Gunnar.

2 By the time Hugo arrived, the snack bar was out of hot dogs.

3 Ursula, who was the first to arrive, enjoyed a cold treat.

4 Nora was thirsty after enjoying her salty treat.

wall art

Make your way around the paintings from START to FINISH.

maze

FINISH

START HERE

wrench

golf club

orange slice

glasses

doughnut

bow

pizza slice

banana

domino

sweet invention

Sylvester the cat scientist has created the perfect machine to get his pet *T. rex* her cookies. Can you find the 15 hidden objects in the scene? Can you also find 6 milk cartons?

horseshoe

envelope

hot dog

button

ring

sock

SUMS AND SLICES

Each of these 4 slices of pizza should have the numbers 1 through 6 running along its edges. Each of the sides must add up to the number in the middle of the slice. Can you place the missing numbers so that everything adds up correctly?

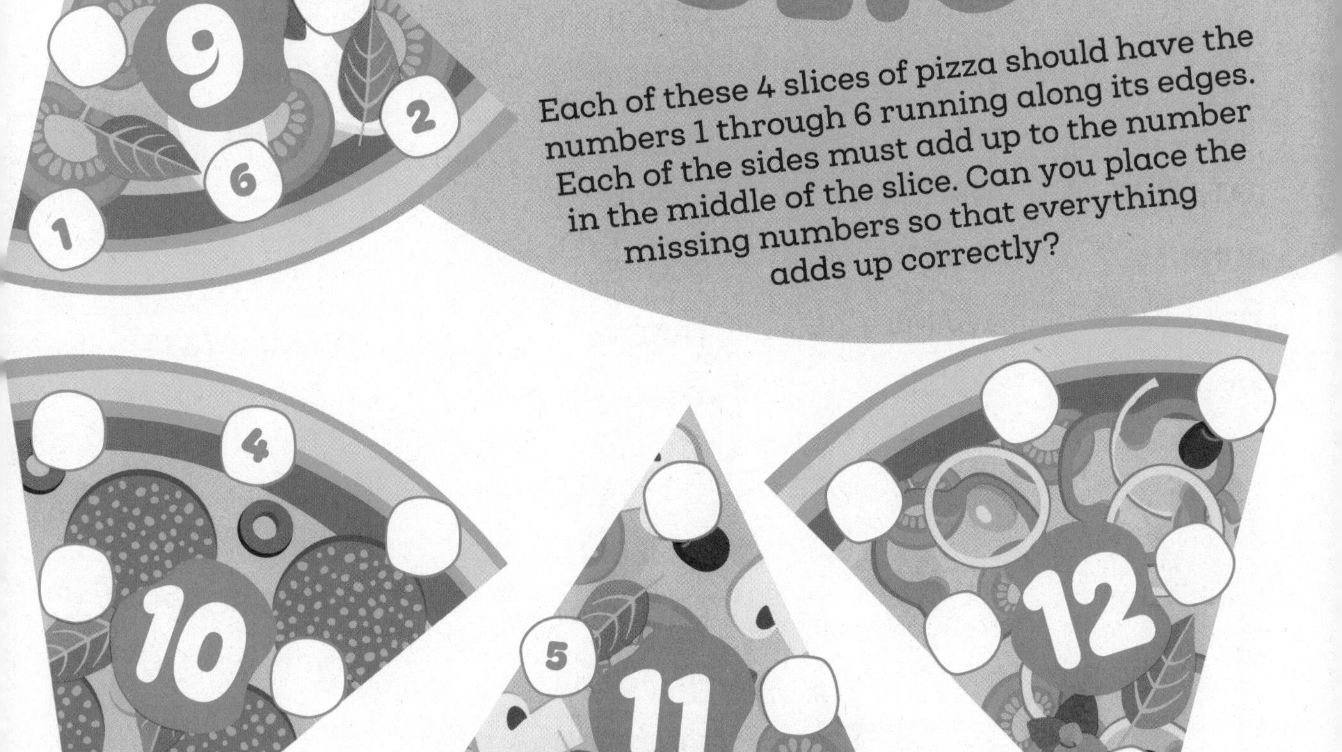

Slice 1: 3, 9, 2, 6, 1

Slice 2 (center 10): 4, 3

Slice 3 (center 11): 5

Slice 4 (center 12)

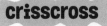

GO TEAM!

It's game time! These 35 words about sports fit together in the grid in only one way. Use the size of each word as a clue to where it might fit. We started you off with BALL.

WORD LIST

3 LETTERS

BAT
RUN
TIE
WIN

4 LETTERS

BALL
FANS
GAME
GOAL
JUMP
LOSE
TEAM

5 LETTERS

CATCH
COURT
FIELD
GLOVE
SCORE
THROW

6 LETTERS

CHEERS
POINTS
SOCCER
TROPHY
UMPIRE

7 LETTERS

JERSEYS
REFEREE

8 LETTERS

BASEBALL
FOOTBALL
HALFTIME
PRACTICE
SOFTBALL
TRAINING

9 LETTERS

TEAMMATES

10 LETTERS

BASKETBALL
SCOREBOARD
TOURNAMENT

12 LETTERS

CHAMPIONSHIP

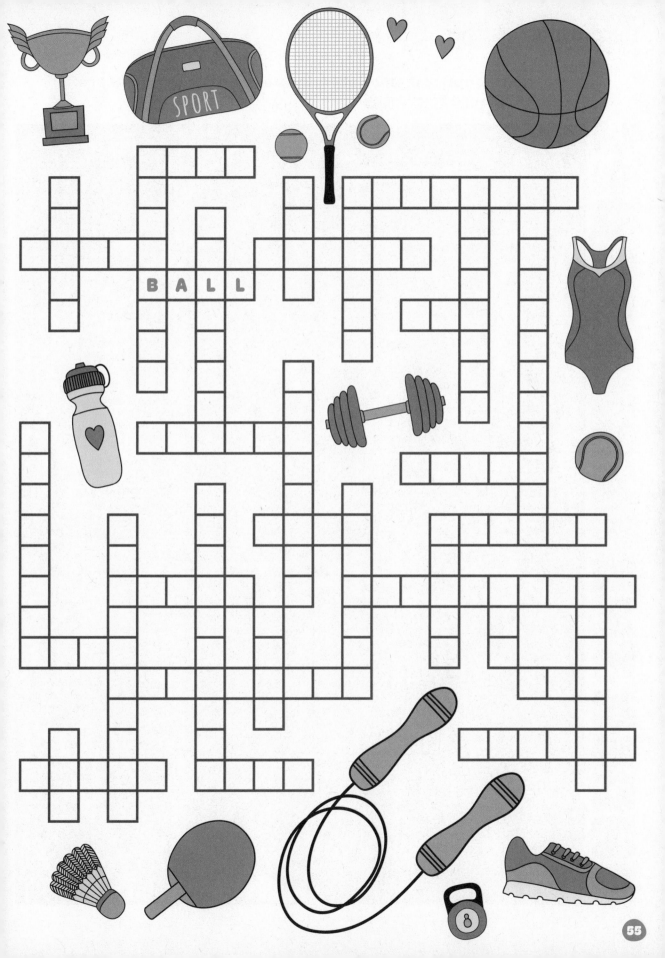

BALL

This micrograph of a pine-tree trunk is hiding 14 toothbrushes. Without using a microscope, see if you can find them.

UNDER THE MICROSCOPE

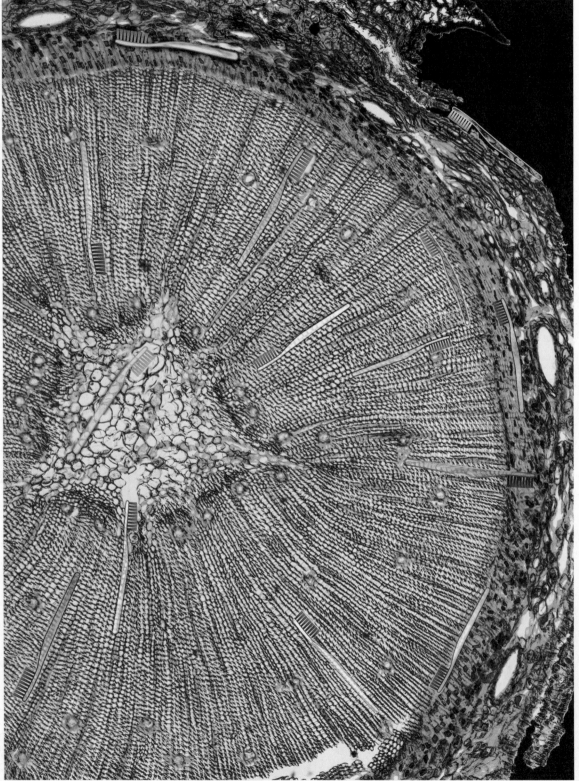

a gaggle of giraffes

Find the impostor in this group of giraffes. It has a hump and lives in the desert. Can you also find 11 red bow ties?

WACKY WORDS

All the wacky words below are real terms. Can you match each one to its definition?

1. ___ BAMBOOZLE

2. ___ SMAZE

3. ___ MELDROP

4. ___ BUMBERSHOOT

5. ___ OBELUS

6. ___ BEEF

7. ___ LOLLYGAG

8. ___ POIPOLE

9. ___ NAUSEANT

10. ___ QUIRE

A. A drop of snot coming from the nose

B. The math sign for division

C. Something that causes nausea

D. A combo of smoke and haze

E. Another word for *umbrella*

F. Waste time or dawdle

G. Deceive

H. A choppy sea

I. A half-acre plot of land

J. About two dozen sheets of paper

cactus patterns

Find each pattern below in the grid.

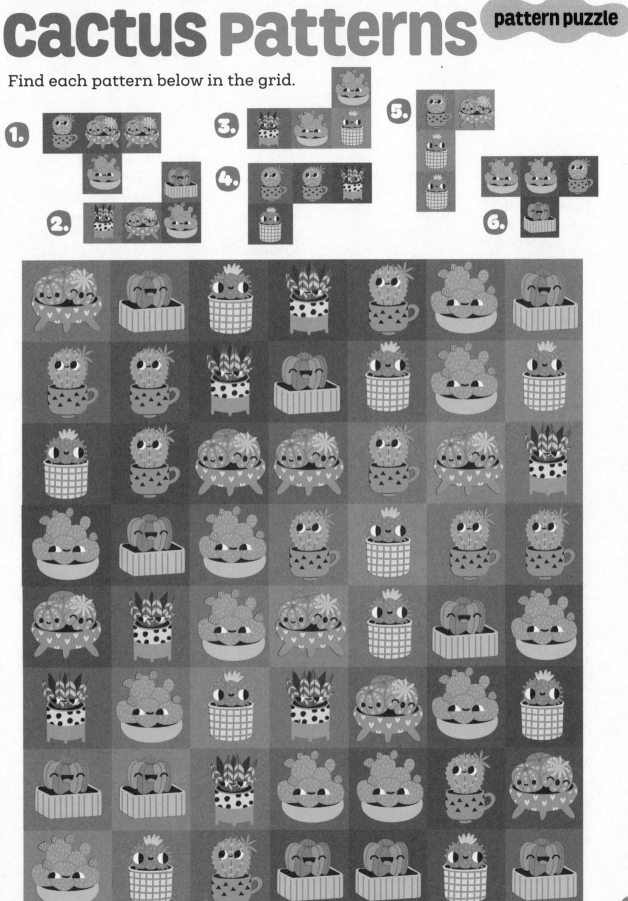

59

one odd airport

Study this wacky scene for two minutes. Then cover up everything except the pink section below and try to answer the questions.

HL-TV

TAKEOFF AIRPORT

GATES 9 3/4

WALDO THE GREAT

cheese

TAXI

TEST YOUR MEMORY!

1. What is the name of this airport?
2. What unusual passengers are riding in the taxi?
3. Which prehistoric creature is soaring above the airport?
4. Which prickly plant is growing from the airport roof?
5. What is the scuba diver holding under her arm?

TRICKY STACKS

Look closely at the stacks below. Can you figure out how many shipping containers are in each stack?

1.
2.
3.
4.
5.
6.

HINT: Some containers are hidden beneath or behind other containers.

SOCKS galore!

Each sock has an exact match. Can you find all 10 pairs?

STICK BUG ART CLASS

BONUS!
Can you also find the ruler, horseshoe, domino, and banana?

adhesive bandage

thermometer

boomerang

button

hockey stick

slice of pie

paddle

toothbrush

jelly bean

rolling pin

handbroom

top hat

thermos

hammer

lollipop

flashlight

paper clip

screw

cotton swab

drumstick

ice-cream scoop

thumbtack

gimme space!

Test how much you know about space with an out-of-this-world quiz.

1. Pluto is known as this.
   a. A dwarf planet
   b. A baby planet
   c. A puppy planet

2. Which planet is closest to the sun?
   a. Mercury
   b. Venus
   c. Earth

3. How much bigger is the sun's diameter than Earth's?
   a. 19 times bigger
   b. 109 times bigger
   c. 19 million times bigger

4. What are Saturn's rings made of?
   a. Ice, dust, and rocks
   b. Fiery gas
   c. Gold and diamonds

5. A quasar is:
   a. Far away and very bright
   b. Far away and very dark
   c. Afraid of the dark

6. What year did astronauts first walk on the moon?
   a. 1949
   b. 1969
   c. 1999

7. What is a common nickname for Mars?
   a. The Red Planet
   b. The Green Planet
   c. E.T.'s Home Planet

8. What is the name of Jupiter's largest moon?
   a. Mimas
   b. Bigby
   c. Ganymede

9. How many known comets are in our solar system?
   a. Less than 200
   b. More than 3,800
   c. About 9.2 million

10. How long is a day on Neptune?
   a. About 11 hours
   b. About 16 hours
   c. About 25 hours

say this five times, fast: Surely Shirley should start to study stars.

BIKE RACE

Compare these two pictures of animals biking across the savanna.
Can you find at least 25 differences?

ARCTIC ANIMAL SEARCH

The names of 19 animals that you might find in the Arctic
are hidden in the grid. Can you find them all?

WORD LIST

- ARCTIC FOX
- ARCTIC WOLF
- CARIBOU
- DALL SHEEP
- ELK
- GRAY WHALE
- HARP SEAL
- LYNX
- MINK
- MOOSE
- MUSK OX
- NARWHAL
- POLAR BEAR
- PTARMIGAN
- PUFFIN
- SNOWSHOE HARE
- SNOWY OWL
- WALRUS
- WOLVERINE

```
E E C A R I B O U G W S V
R L R A R C T I C W O L F
A H Y R Q V E R O M T E R
E A E N I R E V L O W P M
B H V A X H X O K S U M A
R A G R A Y W H A L E Q R
A R Z E A T N R T L E M C
L P B N A G I M R A T P T
O S I X H Q D I K M G G I
P E E H S L L A D N A Q C
K A P U F F I N F O I O F
E L K S Z Z H C A J V M O
Q L W O Y W O N S L W R X
S N O W S H O E H A R E H
F L A H W R A N E S O O M
L B Z V K S W A L R U S R
```

tasty toast
sudoku

Every slice of toast should only appear once in each row, column, and 2 × 3 box. Fill in the squares by drawing each slice or by writing the number.

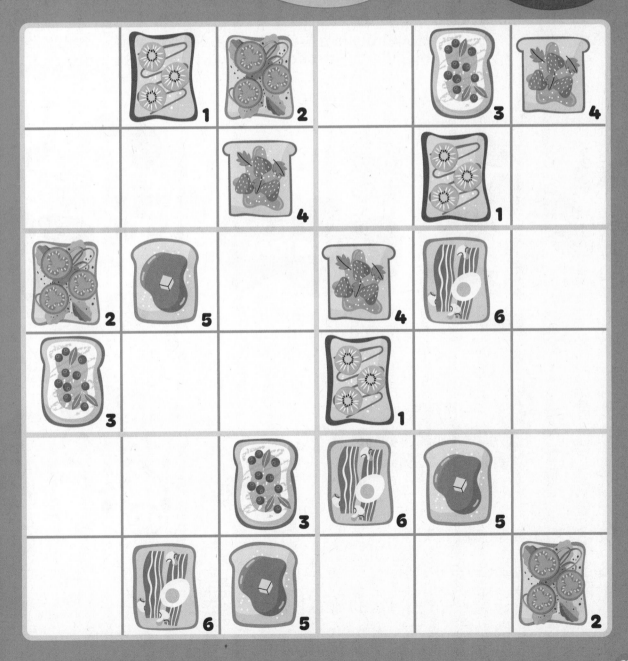

FIND THE PATTERN

Each snowflake is missing one side. Can you match the missing side to the snowflake with the same pattern?

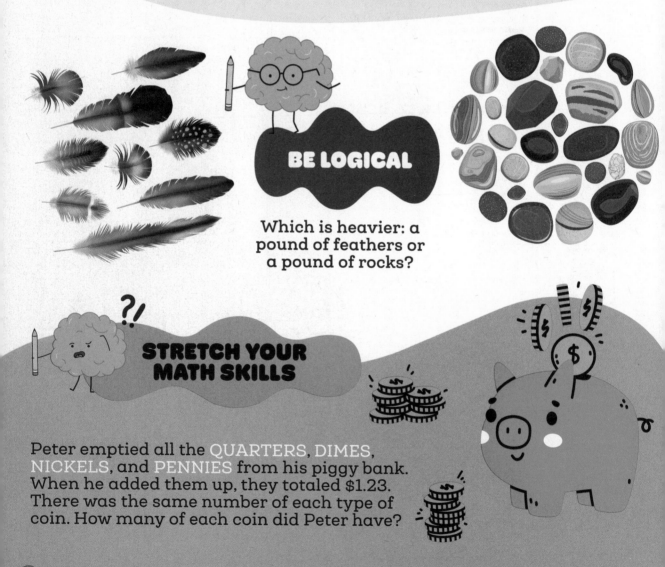

BE LOGICAL

Which is heavier: a pound of feathers or a pound of rocks?

STRETCH YOUR MATH SKILLS

Peter emptied all the QUARTERS, DIMES, NICKELS, and PENNIES from his piggy bank. When he added them up, they totaled $1.23. There was the same number of each type of coin. How many of each coin did Peter have?

HINT: Quick, grab some tissues!

TEST YOUR EYESIGHT

WHAT IS THIS?

HA HA !!

TICKLE YOUR FUNNY BONE

Which knight was best at jousting?

Lance-lot.

He added up the numbers.

The water tank leaked.

DO A WORD WORKOUT

Dad went to every game.

Find the body part hidden in each sentence. EXAMPLE: Mike wore yellow shoes.

She left both umbrellas at home.

Should Erin leave later?

We went to the beach in Mom's car.

ALPINE ADVENTURES

Without clues or knowing what to look for, can you find the 25 hidden objects at this mountain resort?

which mountain is the sleepiest?

Mount Ever-rest.

CANDY COUNTER

Each type of treat costs less than 10 cents. Can you look at these prices and figure out how much each kind costs?

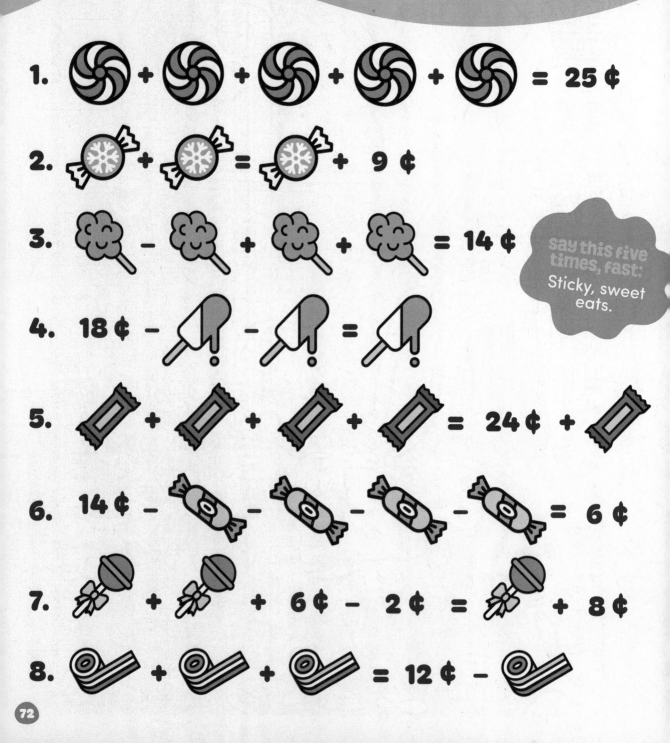

1. 🍬 + 🍬 + 🍬 + 🍬 + 🍬 = 25 ¢

2. 🍬 + 🍬 = 🍬 + 9 ¢

3. 🍭 − 🍭 + 🍭 + 🍭 = 14 ¢

say this five times, fast: Sticky, sweet eats.

4. 18 ¢ − 🍦 − 🍦 = 🍦

5. 🍫 + 🍫 + 🍫 + 🍫 = 24 ¢ + 🍫

6. 14 ¢ − 🍬 − 🍬 − 🍬 − 🍬 = 6 ¢

7. 🍭 + 🍭 + 6¢ − 2¢ = 🍭 + 8 ¢

8. 🍥 + 🍥 + 🍥 = 12 ¢ − 🍥

middle ages mix-up

This picture shows a scene from the Middle Ages in Europe, which was from about the 5th century to the 15th century. There's one problem, though. Some items in the picture hadn't been invented yet. Can you spot at least 10 items that are not in the right time?

BBQ CROSSWORD

Warning—some of the yummy answers in this crossword puzzle might make your mouth water! Use the clues to fill in the puzzle.

ACROSS

✓ 1. Just plain dull; rhymes with *crab*

5. Opposite of happy

8. Male sibling of Sis

11. Like the floor of an auto repair shop, or like unwashed hair

12. Ginger_____ (soft drink)

13. Smack with an open hand

14. Side dish served at a barbecue

16. "This game is not fair. I___!"

17. Yellow transport to school

18. "Don't let the toast_____."

19. "Small" barbecue meat that falls off the bone (3 words)

24. Astrological sign for someone born between late March and late April

25. Group of cattle or horses

26. Color on a stoplight

27. Purchase from a store

28. Make the lights less bright

31. Two of a kind; a ___ of socks

33. Set of beliefs

35. Yellow vegetable served at a barbecue (4 words)

38. _____ , Dewey, and Louie

39. Get _____ of (discard)

40. Songs on the charts

41. Cold dessert served at a barbecue (2 words)

46. Another word for dollar bills

47. Two thousand pounds

48. One of the Great Lakes

49. Black paving material used on roads

50. Covering for a lawn's bald spot

51. Alert someone about a danger

DOWN

1. "What's up, _____ ?"; rhymes with *rock*

2. _____ de Janeiro, Brazil

3. "I'm _____ ears."

4. "So long!"

5. Spicy taco topping or dip

6. Pie ___ ___ mode (2 words)

7. Moisture on the grass in the morning

8. Book jacket quote; rhymes with *herb*

9. "When it _____, it pours."

10. Choose

13. Underwater creature that squirts ink

15. Underwater boats

18. "It's c-c-cold!"

19. Candy _____

20. "____you sure about that?"

21. Take part in an auction

22. It was once common for people to_____ their own butter.

23. It unlocks the door

27. Person's life story (abbreviation)

28. Christmas's month (abbreviation)

29. "What can ___ ___ for you?" (2 words)

30. Out-of-control crowd

31. ____the button in the elevator

32. Not in _____ way, shape, or form

33. Stylish and sophisticated; rhymes with *beak*

34. Did a sketch over again

35. Country with the Great Wall

36. _____ space (rocket ship's destination)

37. When a style becomes popular, it's the latest _____ .

40. Cold's opposite

41. "_____ a long story."

42. Pigeon's call, or baby's sound

43. Stat for a pitcher (abbreviation)

44. Balloon contents

45. Dads and uncles, for example

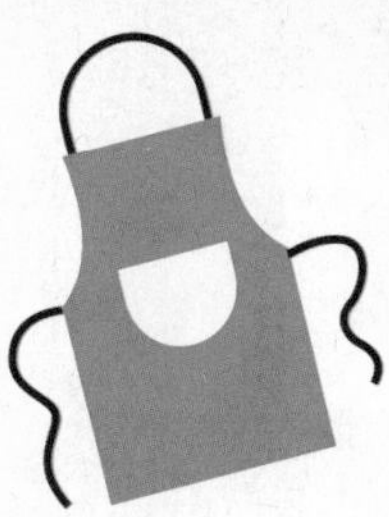
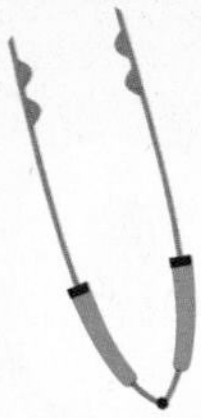
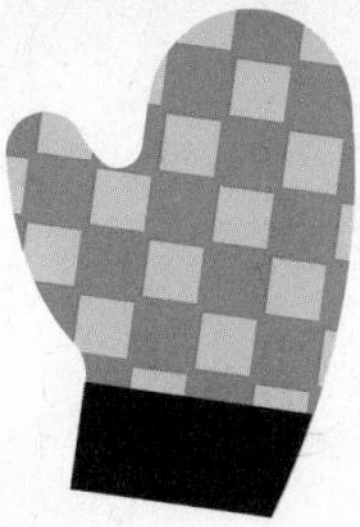
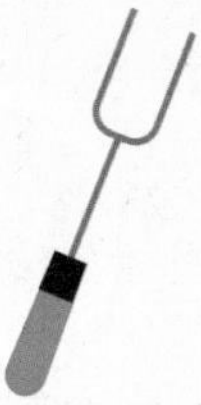

HINT! If you don't know the answer to a clue, look at the other clues that are around it, both across and down, or try another part of the puzzle and come back to the tough clue later.

1 D	2 R	3 A	4 B	■	5	6	7	■	■	8	9	10
11				■	12			■	13			
14				15				■	16			
■	■	■	17			■	■	18				■
19	20	21				22	23					■
24					■	25				■	■	■
26			■	■	27			■	■	28	29	30
■	■	■	31	32			■	33	34			
■	35	36					37					
■	38				■	■	39			■	■	■
40				■	41	42				43	44	45
46				■	47			■	48			
49			■	■	50			■	51			

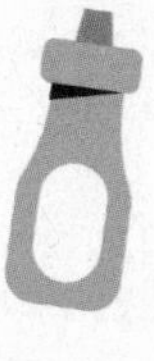
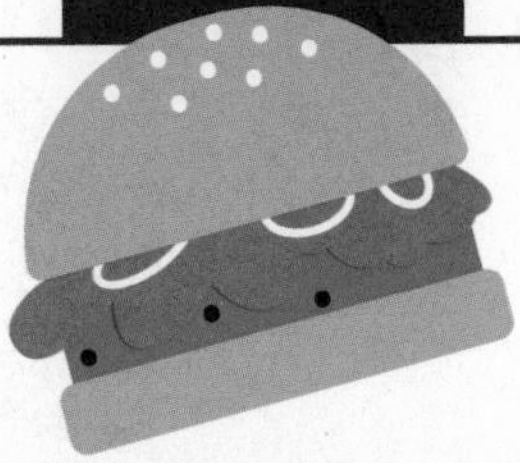
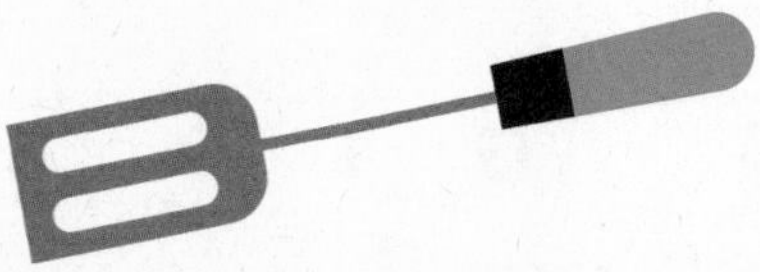
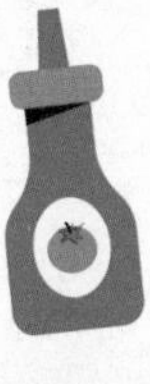

frog code

Ready for an un-frog-ettable challenge? Follow the directions below to crack the code and reveal a tongue twister. Then see if you can say it five times fast.

1. Change each **G** to the letter that comes before it in the alphabet.

2. Change the **Y** to the twenty-first letter in the alphabet.

3. Change each **B** to a letter that sounds like a hot drink.

4. Change each **H** to the seventh letter in the alphabet.

5. Every time you see a **P**, change it to two letters after **Q**.

6. Change each **K** to a letter that is perfectly round.

7. When you see the **N**, change it to the next-to-last letter in the alphabet.

8. Change each **D** to three letters before **U**.

9. Every time you see an **L**, change it to the last vowel in the word *croak*.

10. Change the **F** to the letter after **M**.

11. Change the **W** to the letter that sounds like a part of the face.

12. Change the **R** to the letter between **O** and **Q**.

13. Change the **X** to the letter that rhymes with *tell*.

$$\underline{G} \quad \underline{K} \quad \underline{Y} \quad \underline{D} \qquad \underline{G} \quad \underline{L} \quad \underline{P} \quad \underline{B}$$

$$\underline{G} \quad \underline{D} \quad \underline{K} \quad \underline{H} \quad \underline{P} \qquad \underline{G} \quad \underline{X} \quad \underline{N} \quad \underline{W} \quad \underline{F} \quad \underline{H}$$

$$\underline{R} \quad \underline{L} \quad \underline{P} \quad \underline{B} \qquad \underline{G} \quad \underline{L} \quad \underline{P} \quad \underline{B}.$$

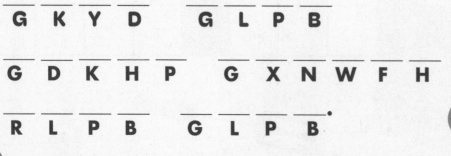

shadow match

Look at the shadows. Match each one to the correct building below.

1. 2. 3. 4. 5. 6. 7. 8.

snack PATH

It's snack time! But before you can snag your treat, you have to find the correct path through this vending machine. Figure out how to get from ENTER to EXIT, passing beneath the numbers 5, 10, 15, 20, and 25 in order without backtracking or repeating any routes.

penguins with pucks

Can you find the camera, television, chess game, magician's wand, cat, playing card, zebra, soccer ball, earmuffs, tuxedo, skunk, newspaper, dalmatian, baseball cap, and 8 ball? Can you also find 5 black-and-white cookies?

CHECK THEM!

EITHER TEAM!

GO REFS!

HI MOM

B&W Pianos

GRAYMAN TIRES

79

BEE CAREFUL

Figure out where these 10 pieces go in the puzzle.

1.
2.
3.
4.
5.
6.
7.
8.
9.
10.

A.
B.
C.
D.
E.
F.
G.
H.
I.
J.

Ready, set, GO!

In this scene, 10 items have been replaced by a rhyming item. For example, a seat has been replaced by a beet. How many others can you find? Can you also find 8 things that rhyme with *go*?

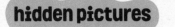

super-duper pancake maker

slice of
cheese

vase

pretzel

chef's
hat

hockey
stick

comb

ax

it's a WRAP

Lola's friends surprised her with a birthday party and presents. But they forgot to put tags on the gifts. Using the clues below, can you figure out which friend gave Lola which gift?

	Amber	Billy	Chad	Daphne
red gift				
blue gift				
yellow gift				
green gift				
red bow				
blue bow				
yellow bow				
green bow				

Use the chart to keep track of your answers. Put an **X** in each box that can't be true and an **O** in boxes that match.

CLUES

1 No gift has the same color wrapping paper and ribbon.

2 A girl brought a yellow gift with a red bow.

3 Billy did not put a green bow on his gift.

4 Amber did not bring a red bow or gift.

5 Billy used his favorite color, blue, to wrap his gift.

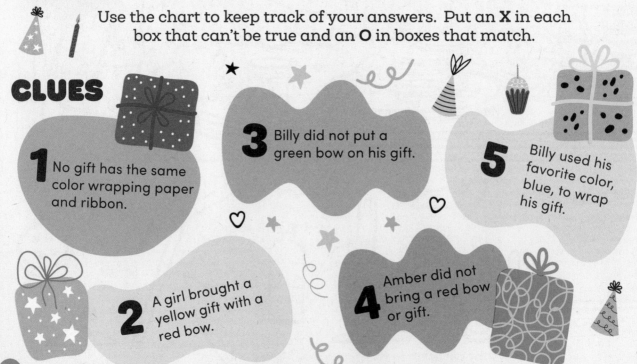

tree trails

Help Antonia move from START to FINISH along the branches.

maze

START

FINISH

BONUS

Write down the letters you pass along the right path to answer the riddle:

WHAT IS THE BIGGEST ANT IN THE WORLD?

_ _ _ _ _ _ _ _ _ _ _

AUSSIE ANIMALS

G'day, mate! Australia is home to many fascinating animals. Thirty-four of them are hiding "down under" in this grid. Look up, down, across, backward, and diagonally to find the words. Ready? Hop to it!

WORD LIST

~~AMPUTA~~	EMU	PILLIGA MOUSE
BANDICOOT	FAIRY PENGUIN	POTOROO
BILBY	FLYING FOX	QUOKKA
BLACK SWAN	GHOST BAT	SKINK
BROLGA	KANGAROO	SUGAR GLIDER
CASSOWARY	KOALA	TASMANIAN DEVIL
COCKATOO	KOOKABURRA	WALLABY
CROCODILE	KOWARI	WALLAROO
DIBBLER	LACE MONITOR	WOMBAT
DINGO	LORIKEET	YABBY
DUGONG	MULGARA	
ECHIDNA	NUMBAT	

```
B W B L A C E M O N I T O R D T I
R I E C H I D N A I Q U O K K A N
O B L H K A B R D U C G O O F B U
E L I B L X A I L G D B O O Q M R
S A D A Y D N L R N N R R K E O S
U C O R P G D O O E W O A A E W R
O K C E O C I R M P A D G B O A M
M S O D T O C I A Y L B N U N L U
A W R I O C O K M R L A A R D L L
G A C L R K O E P I A K K R Y A G
I N B G O A T E U A R A T A R B A
L U M R O T W T T F O W G Y A Y R
L M Y A Q O N O A P O U V L W N A
I B A G J O L A K T A B T S O H G
P A B U O J A K N I K N I K S R I
Q T B S K X D I B B L E R F S N B
F L Y I N G F O X K A B O U A F T
T A S M A N I A N D E V I L C G W
```

farm frenzy

Study this wacky scene for two minutes. Then cover up everything except the red section below and try to answer the questions.

MODOOO

MUNCH MUNCH

#1

#1

Test your memory!

1. What oversize veggie is the pig munching on?
2. What is written on the blimp?
3. What treat is in the back of the pickup truck?
4. What is the cow sitting in on the front porch of the house?
5. What sport is being played outside the barn?

snack attack patterns

Find each pattern below in the grid.

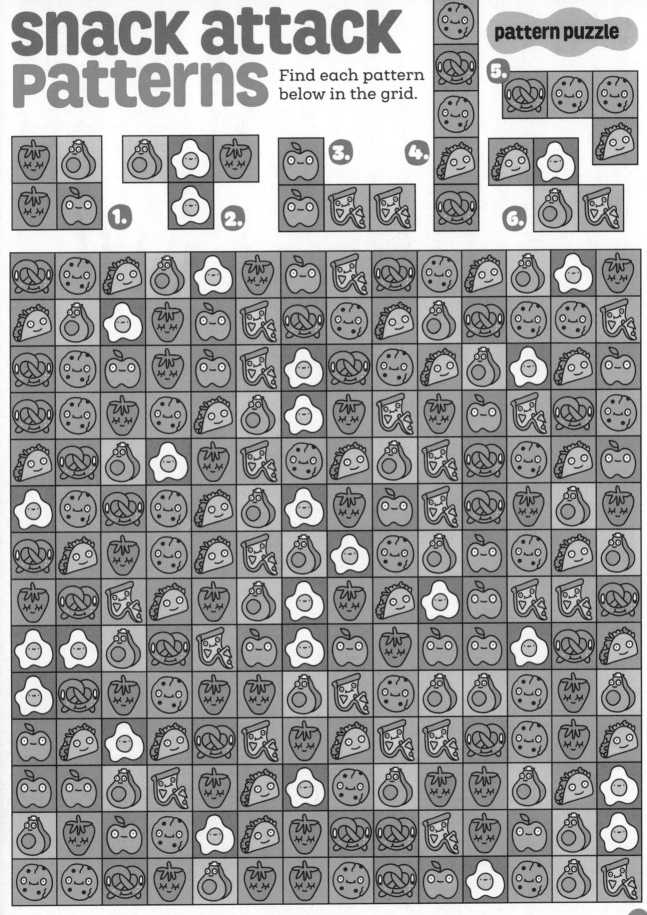

BE LOGICAL

An artist drew a pattern without crossing over or doubling back along any lines. Can you figure out how she did it?

DO A WORD WORKOUT

Find the rhyming equivalent of each of these animal descriptions. Example: A clam who won't share: A selfish shellfish!

Silly hopping mammal

Where a small rodent lives

Wet puppy

Talkative feathered friend

Tiny striped insect

Cautious yellow bird

GUESSTIMATE

Take a look at these fish, but DON'T COUNT THEM! Guess how many are in the group. Afterward, count the fish. How close were you?

TEST YOUR EYESIGHT

HINT: It glows with the flow.

WHAT IS THIS?

TICKLE YOUR FUNNY BONE

What's a dinosaur's favorite drink?

Tea rex.

STRETCH YOUR MATH SKILLS

Two mystery numbers, represented by A and B, work for all four equations. What are the numbers?

$$A + B = 12$$
$$A - B = 8$$
$$A \times B = 20$$
$$A \div B = 5$$

owl sudoku

Every owl should only appear once in each row, column, and 2 × 3 box. Fill in the squares by drawing each owl or by writing the number.

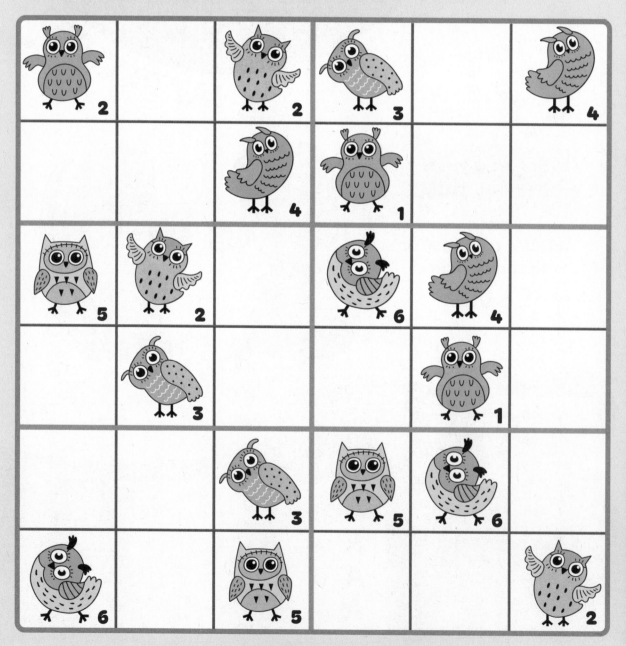

93

HIDE-AND-SEEK

Find at least 20 differences between these two images. Then see if you can spot the item that appears in both images but in a different place.

button SET

Only two buttons are an exact match. Can you find them?

ADOPTION DAY!

Without clues or knowing what to look for, can you
find the 21 objects hidden at this pet adoption fair?

SPORTY SEARCH

Look closely at this picture. Can you find five golf balls, two bowling balls, a pair of goggles, three stopwatches, two volleyballs, a hockey stick, and a whistle? Ready, set, go!

on your LEFT!

Can you find the route through this neighborhood that reaches each house by using 10 straight lines and making only left turns? You can go across, up, down, or diagonally.

START

FINISH

all the avocados

Find the impostor in this bunch of avocados. It's a green and crunchy veggie. Can you also find 12 tortilla chips?

MARCO!

POLO!

CAN YOU TAG THREE SWIMMERS?

1. Hold a pencil at least 12 inches above the page. To tag a player, close your eyes and try to place the pencil point down on anyone in the pool. If you tag a swimmer, place a check mark on them and take another turn. If you don't tag anyone, your turn is over.

2. If you tag someone outside of the pool or sitting on the edge of the pool, you've lost the game. (If you're playing alone, keep trying until you've tagged three swimmers. Can you do it in under eight tries?)

3. Keep playing until one person has tagged three players.

AT THE MOVIES

You might need some popcorn for this movie puzzle.

ACROSS

1. _____ and robbers
✓5. Compact _____, or CDs
10. Song for two
11. Box office purchase
12. Famous actor or actress
13. "Psst!" (2 words)
14. Enthusiastic response to "Who wants to see a movie?" (2 words)
16. Movie snack, often with butter
20. Abbreviation for the Transportation Security Administration
23. To stop, or put an _____ _____ (2 words)
24. Be ready for
26. Hot drink alternative to coffee
27. Type of movie that has a love story
29. "You look familiar. Have we _____?"
30. Intensely ferocious
35. Drink purchased at a movie concession stand
39. Type of movie with chase scenes and explosions
40. Strong, bad smell
41. "_____ or not, here I come!"
42. Adam's apple spot

DOWN

1. Abbreviation for compact discs
2. Opposite of in
3. It's small, green, and grows in a pod
4. Stern; severe
5. Lose, in some video games
6. Like slippery winter weather
7. Cloud's home
8. Abbreviation for a corporate boss
9. Letters between R and V
11. Norse god of thunder; also a superhero
15. Spot for a mail slot and a knocker
16. Animal friend at home
17. Four minus three
18. Abbreviation for personal digital assistant
19. "My last _____ is Smith."
20. Light shade of brown
21. Go get them: "_____ 'em, Rover!"
22. Had some lunch
25. Sherlock Holmes's sidekick
28. Bad sign
30. Opposite of near
31. _____ cubes in 35-Across
32. Abbreviation for rough guess as to when a plane lands
33. Get _____ of (discard)
34. Playfully modest
36. Poem full of praise
37. "What's up, _____?"
38. Noah's _____

HINT! If you don't know the answer to a clue, look at the clues around it, both across and down, or try another part of the puzzle and come back to the tough clue later.

1	2	3	4	■	■	5 D	6 I	7 S	8 C	9 S
10				■	11					
12				■	13					
■	■	■	14	15		■	■	■	■	■
16	17	18				19	■	20	21	22
23					■	24	25			
26			■	27	28					
■	■	■	■	■	29			■	■	■
30	31	32	33	34		■	35	36	37	38
39						■	40			
41					■	■	42			

RAIN OR

To go from this maze's cloudy START to its sunny FINISH, you have to find the one path that takes you through alternating clouds and suns. You may not retrace or cross your path.

START

SHINE

FINISH

BLOCKS ROCK!

Figure out where these 10 pieces go in the puzzle.

1.

2.

3.

4.

5.

6.

7.

8.

9.

10.

A.

B.

C.

D.

E.

F.

G.

H.

I.

J.

ESCAPE-ROOM FUN

BONUS!
Can you also find the goose, pencil, and sock?

pushpin

slice of pizza

mushroom

musical note

pine tree

ring

drinking glass

golf club

tent

butterfly

ruler

marker

umbrella

french fries

spoon

saltshaker

teacup

cupcake

banana

flag

ladle

toothbrush

fishhook

107

Perspective

stadium snapshots

Scan the crowd for photographers. Match each of these photos to the photographer who took it.

BONUS!
Find the videographer who is filming the people on the jumbotron.

THINK ABOUT IT

If monsters were real, what might they be AFRAID of?

When might it NOT be a good idea to wear a hat?

Name some things that are easy to FORGET.

What makes something a SPORT?

BE LOGICAL

These clocks are all wrong! Can you figure out the correct times using the example?
Example: 1:89 would be 2:29.

1. 5:76

2. 11:61

3. 4:83

4. 8:90

?!

STRETCH YOUR MATH SKILLS

What's the highest total you can get by drawing a single straight line through this box?

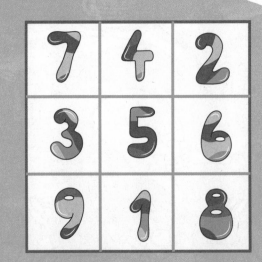

7	4	2
3	5	6
9	1	8

TEST YOUR EYESIGHT

HINT: A one-way ride!

HA HA !!

TICKLE YOUR FUNNY BONE

What are bananas best at in gymnastics?

Splits.

DO A WORD WORKOUT

Use the clues to name words that contain the letters ME.
Example: I am a green fruit: LIME

I am the sound a cat makes.

I am a continent, North or South.

I might be your favorite season.

I am fun to play.

I am the place you live in.

I am a desert animal.

TREE SHADOW

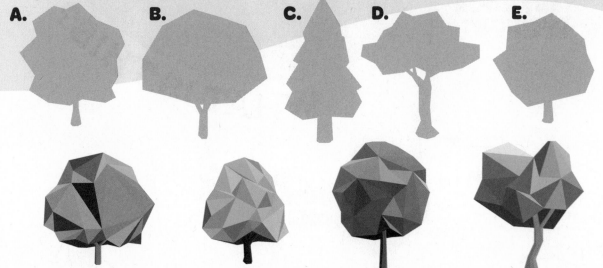

A.   B.   C.   D.   E.

 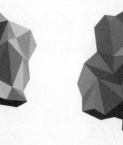  

MATCH

Take a look at the shadows and match each one to the correct tree below.

F.   G.   H.   I.   J.

sea cat circuit

Are they cats? Are they sea creatures? One thing's for sure: They're supercute! Use the sea cat symbols below to figure out the right path through the grid.

Move 1 space — **RIGHT**

Move 1 space — **UP**

Move 1 space

Move 1 space — **DOWN**

Move 1 space — **LEFT**

Move 1 space

PATH 1	PATH 2	PATH 3	PATH 4	PATH 5	PATH 6

EXIT

sprinkle search

These sprinkles are hiding 19 crayons. Can you find them all?

Hiding in the grass

Find the mushroom, four-leaf clover, 14 bugs, a salamander, a tennis ball, 2 snails, a turtle, a frog, 2 snakes, a pea pod, an apple, and a pear.

photo FINISH

Annie and three of her friends entered a photo contest. Using the clues below, can you figure out which photo each took and what prize each won?

	Horse	House	Landscape	Family	1st	2nd	3rd	Honorable Mention
Annie								
George								
Robert								
Sophie								

Use the chart to keep track of your answers. Put an **X** in every box that can't be true and an **O** in boxes that are true.

CLUES

1 One of the friends took a photo of her sister that won 2nd place.

2 The photo that took 1st place was black and white.

3 George's photo of his house showed off the bright blue porch.

4 Sophie is an only child, and she loves to take pictures of mountains.

5 Robert finished ahead of George but behind Sophie.

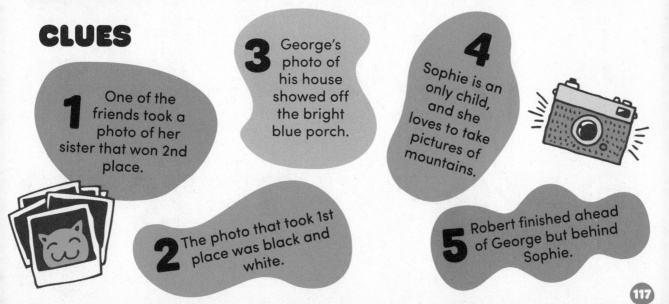

117

BY THE NUMBERS

Start at the 9 in the top left corner. You can move to a new number by adding 4 or subtracting 5. Move up, down, left, or right. Can you make it to the FINISH?

start

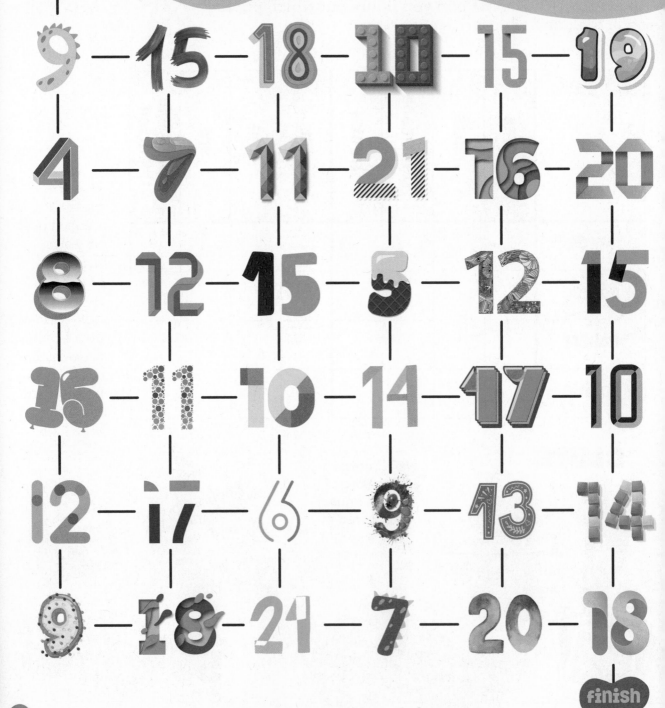

9	15	18	10	15	19
4	7	11	21	16	20
8	12	15	5	12	15
15	11	10	14	17	10
12	17	6	9	13	14
9	18	21	7	20	18

finish

118

slurping snakes

Without clues or knowing what to look for, can you find the 18 hidden objects at Snathan's Noodle Shop?

ocean quiz

Dive deep into this quiz about the oceans.
Read each sentence below and circle **T** if you
think it's true and **F** if you think it's false.

T F **1.** Dolphins can hold their breath for 45 minutes.

T F **2.** Crabs live in every ocean in the world.

T F **3.** Baby blue whales weigh about 3 tons at birth.

T F **4.** The Atlantic Ocean was named after explorer John G. Atlantic.

T F **5.** Seaweed extracts are sometimes used to make ice cream.

T F **6.** Sharks can grow and use over 20,000 teeth in their lifetimes.

T F **7.** All octopuses are venomous.

T F **8.** The largest pearl in the world is called the Pearl of Mulan.

T F **9.** Orcas can live to be 70 years old.

T F **10.** The vampire squid sleeps in coffins and only comes out at night.

T F **11.** In the 18th and 19th centuries, walrus tusks were used to make false teeth.

T F **12.** The longest mountain range in the world is found underwater.

T F **13.** Toronto, Canada, hosts the world-famous statue of the Little Mermaid.

T F **14.** One electric eel can produce enough electricity to light up 10 light bulbs.

T F **15.** Baby harp seals were voted the world's most adorable animals.

supermarket search

You have two minutes to find the items below on your grocery list. Set a timer and see if you can find everything you need in time!

can you find:

SANDY STUMPER

What do the beach spots in each row (horizontally, vertically, and diagonally) have in common?

60-SECOND STUMPER:

You've made a list of items to bring to the beach—but each word has gotten jumbled. Unscramble each word so you can start your fun in the sun!

1. wumitiss

2. etlow

3. drsaufrbo

4. glgoges

5. lfip-ofpls

6. ookb

sports speak

Can you match each sports term above to its definition below? Look closely at the pictures for hints!

1. GOAT
2. Hat trick
3. Ace
4. Lumber
5. Zebra
6. Campfire
7. Traveling
8. Turkey
9. Flea-flicker
10. Spoon

A. When a player scores three goals in the same game.

B. A nickname for a referee due to the black-and-white uniforms they wear.

C. Taking more steps than allowed before dribbling in basketball.

D. An amazing athlete. The "greatest of all time."

E. A wooden baseball bat.

F. A volleyball that falls on the floor and is surrounded by two or more players.

G. A nickname for a lacrosse stick.

H. In tennis or volleyball, a serve that is not returned by the opponent. The server wins that point.

I. Three strikes in a row in bowling.

J. A football play involving a combination of handoffs and forward or lateral passes.

PRIMATE HEAD-SCRATCHER

Each of these primate names fits into the grid in just one way. Use the size of each word as a clue to where it might fit. When you're done, write the letters from the shaded squares in order in the spaces below to see the answer to the riddle.

WORD LIST

3 LETTERS
APE

4 LETTERS
~~DOUC~~

5 LETTERS
LEMUR
LORIS
POTTO

6 LETTERS
AYE-AYE
BABOON
BONOBO
GALAGO
GIBBON
LANGUR
MONKEY

7 LETTERS
COLOBUS
GORILLA
MACAQUE
TAMARIN
TARSIER

8 LETTERS
MANDRILL
MARMOSET

9 LETTERS
ORANGUTAN

10 LETTERS
CHIMPANZEE

RIDDLE
when do gorillas play baseball?

ANSWER: __ __ __ __ __ __ __ - __ __ __ __.

Say this tongue twister five times, fast! **The ape gapes at the grapes.**

DOUC

THERE ARE MORE THAN 200 SPECIES OF PRIMATES!

cookie conundrum

We listed 10 kinds of cookies here. Crack the code to fill in their names. Each number stands for a different letter. Once you know one number's letter, you can fill in that letter in all of the words. Grab some milk and get started!

1. **M A C A R O O N**
   7 10 1 10 1 2 2 8

2. ___ ___ ___ ___ ___   ___ ___ ___
   6 5 7 2 8   9 10 11

3. ___ ___ ___ ___ ___
   13 18 12 10 11

4. ___ ___ ___ ___ ___ ___ ___
   19 2 11 16 18 8 5

5. ___ ___ ___ ___ ___ ___ ___ ___ ___ ___
   12 4 8 12 5 11 13 8 10 14

6. ___ ___ ___ ___ ___ ___ ___ ___ ___ ___
   13 15 2 11 16 9 11 5 10 17

7. ___ ___ ___ ___ ___ ___ ___   ___ ___ ___ ___ ___ ___
   2 10 16 7 5 10 6   11 10 4 13 4 8

8. ___ ___ ___ ___ ___ ___   ___ ___ ___ ___ ___ ___
   14 5 10 8 18 16   9 18 16 16 5 11

9. ___ ___ ___ ___ ___ ___ ___ ___ ___   ___ ___ ___ ___
   1 15 2 1 2 6 10 16 5   1 15 4 14

10. ___ ___ ___ ___ ___ ___ ___ ___ ___ ___ ___ ___ ___
    13 8 4 1 3 5 11 17 2 2 17 6 5

BONUS: WHAT DID THE GINGERBREAD MAN USE TO TRIM HIS FINGERNAILS?

___ ___ ___ ___ ___ ___ ___   ___ ___ ___ ___ ___ ___.
10   1 2 2 3 4 5   1 18 16 16 5 11

zany diner

Study this kooky scene for two minutes. Then cover up everything except the orange section below and try to answer the questions.

OUR MOONCAKES ARE OUT OF THIS WORLD!

Moonbeam DINER

SPECIALS:
GALAXY MELT
METEOR MASH

CHARGING STATION

Test your memory!

1. What's the diner's name?
2. What foods is the UFO in the back beaming up?
3. What are the robot diners pouring on their pancakes?
4. What color is the alien waitress's apron?
5. What type of rodent is hanging from the ceiling?

SNEAKER SEEKERS

It's sale day at the **SNEAKER SHACK**! Twenty-five styles are on display. Almost every sneaker has a perfect match. Can you find the one without a match?

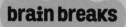

brain breaks

BE LOGICAL

Read these sentences:

1. Today is Alex's birthday.
2. Today is not Alex's birthday.
3. Today is Alexa's birthday.

Only one of these statements can be true. Based on that, can you figure out whether today is Alex's or Alexa's birthday?

DO A WORD WORKOUT

Pancakes, gymnasts, coins

What connects the three things in each group? Example: The ocean, good-byes, sound
Answer: Things with waves.

Unicorns, marching bands, cars

Storms, potatoes, needles

Balloons, corn, bubble gum

Comets, horses, pennies

THINK FAST

How many different vegetables can you name in 60 seconds?

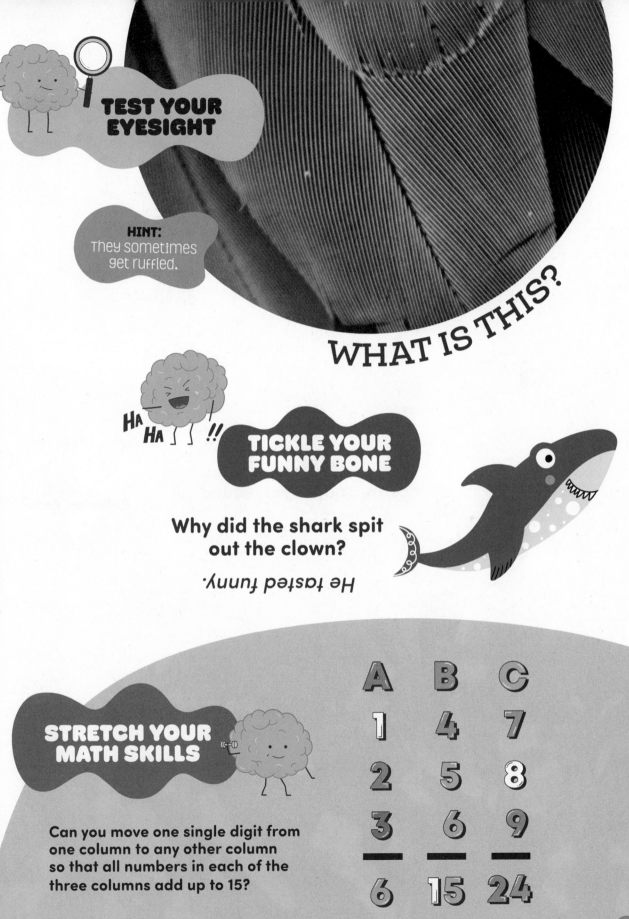

TEST YOUR EYESIGHT

HINT:
They sometimes get ruffled.

WHAT IS THIS?

HA HA !!

TICKLE YOUR FUNNY BONE

Why did the shark spit out the clown?

He tasted funny.

STRETCH YOUR MATH SKILLS

A	B	C
1	4	7
2	5	8
3	6	9
6	15	24

Can you move one single digit from one column to any other column so that all numbers in each of the three columns add up to 15?

COLORFUL CHAOS

In this pile, find 6 bouncy balls, 4 dice, a Rubik's Cube, 5 crayons, 2 rockets, 3 markers, and 6 jacks.

mushroom sudoku

Every mushroom should only appear once in each row, column, and 2 × 3 box. Fill in the squares by drawing each mushroom or writing its number.

Say this tongue twister five times, fast! **Murray messily munched on mushy mushrooms.**

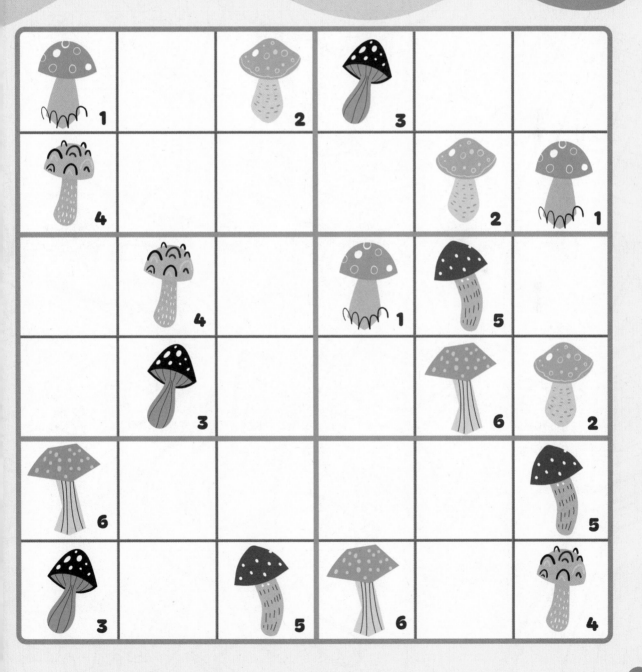

ANIMAL ARCADE

FIND THESE OBJECTS IN THE SCENE.

artist's brush
banana
bell
candle
cherry
crescent moon
crown

envelope
eyeglasses
fishhook
golf club
headphones
hockey stick
horseshoe

ice-cream cone
ladder
lollipop
magnifying
glass
mug
mushroom

nail
needle
ring
ruler
sailboat
saltshaker
shoe

slice of pizza
snake
sock
spool of thread
spoon
snowman
toothbrush

traffic light
T-shirt
wedge of lemon

135

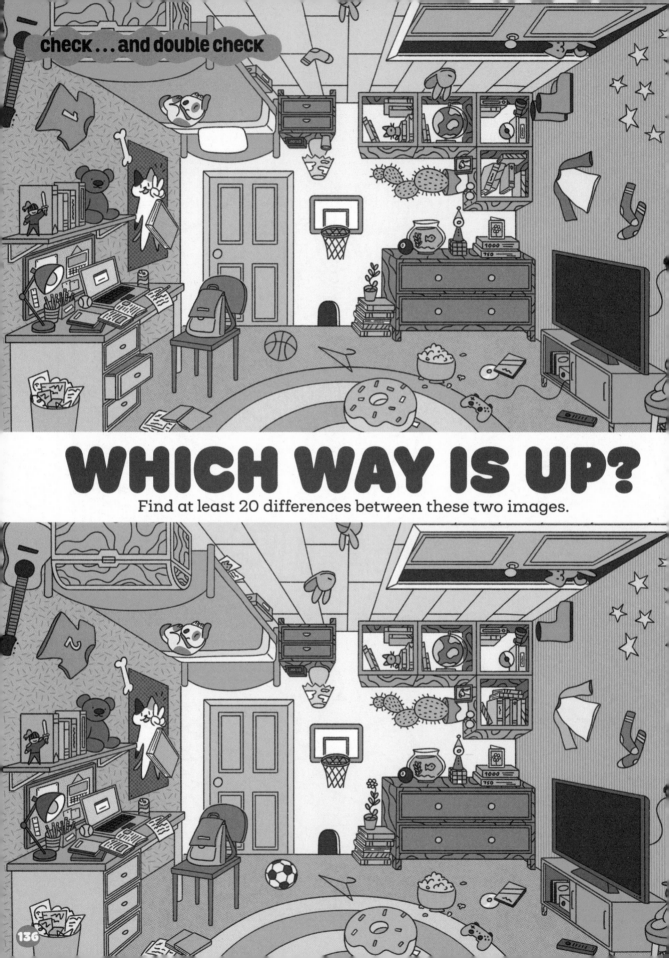

WHICH WAY IS UP?

Find at least 20 differences between these two images.

FISH FEST

his puzzle is pretty fishy! Forty kinds of fish are
wimming in this grid. Look for them up, down, across,
ackward, and diagonally. Can you reel them all in?

```
B P E R C H T U B A R R A C U D A A E
G L S E L N P U W Q E O C E A N N H
R S S C O O O V N D M I N N O W C S
O H A H W M N V N A G B T A N K H I
U S B A N L D A F L O U N D E R O F
P I A L F A Z E S T U R G E O N V R
E F E I I S G O A T F I S H S C Y E
R L S B S W O R D F I S H S E B T F
N E X U H A D D O C K C S I A U B F
M G E T C A T F I S H M A F O A O U
G N I H A M I H A M E M A R L I N P
W A L L E Y E G Y L C S T A P R E I
A I P A L I T N T L A K E T G I F C
S K O E V S T I N G R A Y I U V I K
D J L C H V C R O A K E R U P E S E
O O R A N G E R O U G H Y G P R H R
S L R M A C K E R E L S A Q Y B G E
H K P I K E C H K J H S I F G N U L
```

WORD LIST

ANCHOVY ~~ANCHOVY~~
ANGELFISH
BARRACUDA
BONEFISH
BURI
CARP
CATFISH
CLOWNFISH
CROAKER
FLOUNDER

GOATFISH
GROUPER
GUITARFISH
GUPPY
HADDOCK
HALIBUT
HERRING
LUNGFISH
MACKEREL
MAHI-MAHI

MARLIN
MINNOW
ORANGE ROUGHY
PERCH
PICKEREL
PIKE
PUFFER FISH
SALMON
SEA BASS
SHARK

SMELT
SOLE
STINGRAY
STURGEON
SWORDFISH
TILAPIA
TROUT
TUNA
WALLEYE
ZANDER

137

spacing OUT

Circle sets of four squares that have a rocket, UFO, planet, and satellite. You are done when all the squares are circled.

Each set must have a a rocket, UFO, planet, and satellite.

One side of each square must touch a side of another square in the same set.

cluster of cones

Find the impostor in this group of ice-cream cones. It's a small, frosted treat. Can you also find 10 hidden cherries?

FEATHERY FRACTIONS

Do some math, then get a laugh! Use the fractions of the words listed under the blanks to solve the three bird riddles.

What does a bird with a cold need?

_ _ _ _ _ - _ _ _ _ _

1. First ⅖ of **TWIST**
2. Last ¾ of **FEET**
3. First ⅓ of **MEMORY**
4. Middle ⅓ of **CENTER**

Who leads the bird band?

_ _ _ _ _ _ _ _ _ _ - _ _ _ _ _ _ - _ _ _ _

1. First ⅗ of **THERE**
2. First ⅓ of **COPPER**
3. Last ⅓ of **PEN**
4. First ½ of **DUST**
5. Last ⅖ of **CLOCK**
6. First ¾ of **TORN**

Which bird is best at eating?

_ _ _ _ _ _ _ _ _ _

1. Middle ⅓ of **BAT**
2. First ⅖ of **SWEET**
3. Last ⅓ of **SPA**
4. Last ½ of **TELL**
5. First ⅔ of **OWE**

prairie dog **hotel**

Help Petunia the prairie dog find her way to her room at the Prairie Dog Hotel. Then find 3 keys, 2 ants, 2 mice, a worm, and a lost boot.

start

HOTEL

finish

jigsaw challenge
butterfly bonanza

Figure out where these 10 pieces go in the puzzle.

JELLY JAMBOREE

Grape Jelly and her band The Preserves are jamming out in front of their adoring fans. Can you find 8 words (NOT pictures!) hidden in the scene?

BONUS! Can you also find 5 hidden music notes?

143

BATTER UP

Without clues or knowing what to look for, can you find the 23 hidden objects in this scene?

skateboard LOGIC

Dillon, Reese, Andrew, and Anna went skateboard shopping. Using the clues below, can you figure out what color skateboard each bought and how much each spent?

Use the chart to keep track of your answers. Put an **X** in every box that can't be true and an **O** in boxes that match.

	Dillon	Reese	Andrew	Anna
yellow				
blue				
purple				
orange				
$50				
$60				
$70				
$80				

CLUES

1 Anna spent $10 more than Reese and $10 less than Andrew.

2 Andrew doesn't like yellow.

3 Dillon gave the cashier $100 and got $20 back in change when he bought his purple skateboard.

4 Reese bought a skateboard that matched her blue eyes.

NICE ICE

The icy pond surface looks like a mirror. But some objects are missing in the reflection. Can you find at least 12?

BONUS! At this llama PJ party, there's a king on a swing and a bat with a hat. Can you find at least 3 other rhyming things in the scene?

IT'S CAMPY!

Use the clues to fill in the answers in this crossword puzzle. Every answer has something to do with camping. We did one to get you started.

ACROSS

5. A bottle or canteen holds this.

7. These hold up the tent.

8. Masked animals that come out at night

10. Make a wish on these.

11. A walk through the woods

13. Carry your supplies in this.

15. These birds are awake at night.

18. This keeps mosquitoes away. (two words)

19. You might wear these on an 11 Across.

20. Put this in a cooler to chill food.

21. Bring your rod and reel for this.

22. Treats made from marshmallows, chocolate, and graham crackers

DOWN

1. Gather this for a fire.

2. A lunar night-light

3. Camping shelter

4. Carry this to see at night.

6. Animal footprints

9. Your camping "bed." (two words)

10. Slide marshmallows onto this for roasting.

12. Small, narrow boat

14. You might cook hot dogs over this.

16. What you tell around a 14 Down.

17. You might go swimming here.

BONUS: After you finish the crossword, fill in the spaces below in order from top to bottom and left to right to see the answer to this riddle:

what do octopuses take on camping trips?

ANSWER: __ __ __ __ __-__ __ __ __ __ __ .

5. WATER

THINK ABOUT IT

What are some ways animals use their TAILS?

Would you be you if you had a DIFFERENT NAME?

If you had to spend the night in the woods, would you rather have WALLS OR A ROOF?

BE LOGICAL

Chef Noodle cooks pizza but not pasta. He'll eat jelly but not jam, carrots but not celery, and beef but never ham. He makes a great grilled cheese and a tasty apple pie, but he'd never bake a chocolate cake. CAN YOU TELL WHY?

STRETCH YOUR MATH SKILLS

Can you fill in the blanks in these equations with the numbers from 0 to 9? Each number will be used only once. Hint: Number 6 is used in the equation E.

A. _____ + _____ = 14

B. _____ × _____ = 12

C. _____ + _____ = 10

D. _____ + _____ = 8

E. _____ + _____ = 6

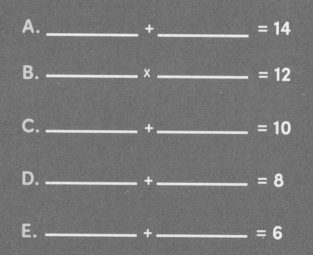

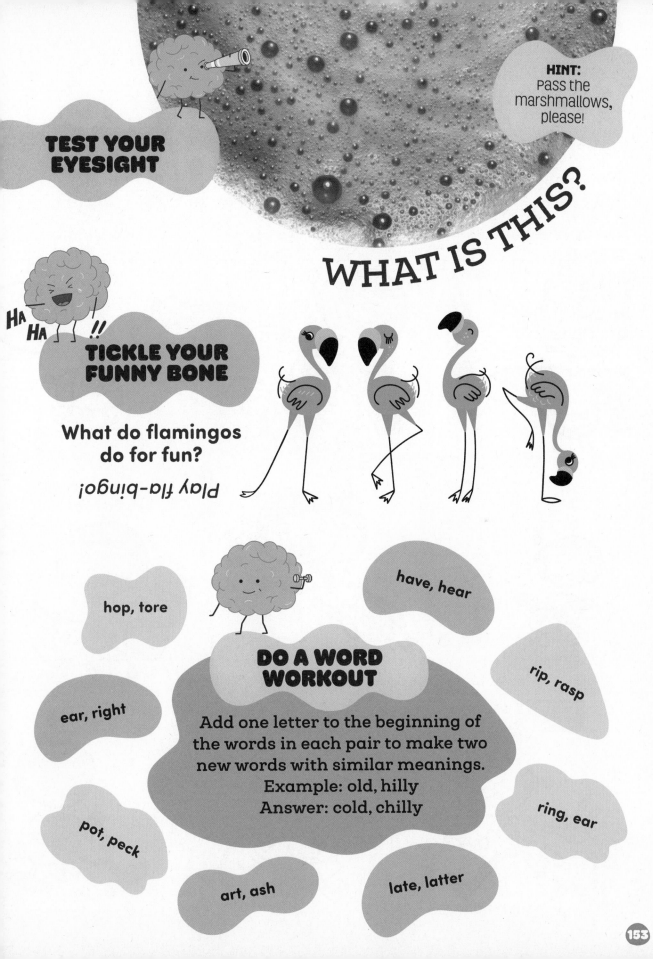

TEST YOUR EYESIGHT

HINT:
Pass the marshmallows, please!

WHAT IS THIS?

HA HA !!

TICKLE YOUR FUNNY BONE

What do flamingos do for fun?

Play fla-bingo!

hop, tore

have, hear

rip, rasp

ear, right

DO A WORD WORKOUT

Add one letter to the beginning of the words in each pair to make two new words with similar meanings.
Example: old, hilly
Answer: cold, chilly

ring, ear

pot, peck

art, ash

late, latter

gizmo and gertie's BOT-TACULAR day

GIZMO'S DAY

Gizmo and Gertie each had a busy day. Can you figure out the order of events for each of them?

BONUS! Gizmo and Gertie almost cross paths while out on their adventures. Can you figure out what time this was?

GERTIE'S DAY

sit. stay. snack!

This popcorn is hiding 20 dog bones. Can you find them all?

People have been eating popcorn for thousands of years!

TASTY LETTERS

Add one letter to the beginning of each word to turn it into a food. For example, add an r to number 1 to get rice.

1. ice
2. read
3. ear
4. live
5. hips
6. oodles
7. each
8. rune

the case of the
CREEPY CRAWLY

Can you track down the creepy crawly who:

- is wearing a hat
- is holding a sugary treat
- doesn't have a blue sweater
- has antennae
- isn't wearing glasses
- has fewer than four eyes

RED PANDA EXTRAVAGANZA

Can you find 2 basketballs, 4 tomatoes, a red squirrel, a fire hydrant, 2 traffic cones, a slice of red velvet cake, a checkers set, 2 red pandas wearing identical hats, and 3 things that rhyme with the word RED?

THAT'S A LOTTA AXOLOTLS!

In two minutes or less, can you find the two columns with the exact same axolotls?

60-SECOND STUMPER

The letters in AXOLOTL can be used to make other words. Use the clues to come up with a few.

1. A ring-shaped island: _ _ _ _ _

2. A hammer is one: _ _ _ _

3. Opposite of short: _ _ _ _

4. Cars can park in one: _ _ _

leafy
labyrinth

Can you be-leaf how tough
this maze is?! See if you can
follow the white line
from START
to FINISH.

maze

start

finish

GET CRAFTY

Place these 35 crafty words or phrases into the grid. They fit together in only one way. Use the number of letters in each word as a clue to where it might fit. We did one to get you started.

WORD LIST

3 LETTERS

SEW

7 LETTERS

CERAMIC

CRAYONS

DRAWING

GLITTER

MARKERS

PASTELS

PENCILS

4 LETTERS

CLAY

FELT

GLUE

PENS

TAPE

YARN

5 LETTERS

BEADS

BRUSH

CHALK

EASEL

FRAME

GLAZE

PAINT

PAPER

8 LETTERS

BUILDING

KNITTING

SCISSORS

STENCILS

STICKERS

6 LETTERS

FABRIC

RIBBON

STAMPS

STICKS

STRING

9 LETTERS

SCRAPBOOK

11 LETTERS

POSTER BOARD

WATERCOLORS

S T E N C I L S

BONUS: After you finish the crossword,
fill in the spaces below in order from top to bottom
and left to right to see the answer to the riddle.

what's blue and smells like green paint?

ANSWER: ___ ___ ___ ___ ___ ___   ___ ___ ___ ___ ___ ___ ___

FLYING SQUIRRELS

BONUS!
Can you also find the football, baseball bat, coat hanger, and sock?

bowl

boomerang

sunglasses

hat

piece of popcorn

crescent moon

crown

comb

carrot

envelope

sailboat

ruler

garden hose

music note

artist's brush

traffic light

banana

fishhook

toothbrush

canoe

heart

hockey stick

mushroom

classic duos

Can you figure out which of these items go together to create classic pairings? There are 12 pairs in all. For each one you find, write down the name of the duo in one of the spaces below. We've done the first one for you.

PEANUT
BUTTER
AND JELLY

NIGHT AND DAY

These images show a daytime and a nighttime scene in the same forest. At night, the sky is dark and the moon is out, of course. But can you find at least 15 other differences between the scenes?

sleep quizzz

See how many questions about sleep you can answer correctly before your bedtime.

1. Which of these refers to sleep?
   a. 40 winks
   b. 40 blinks
   c. 40 lynx

2. About how much of a human's life is spent sleeping?
   a. $\frac{1}{3}$
   b. $\frac{2}{3}$
   c. $\frac{3}{3}$

3. Which of these is a stage of sleep?
   a. INXS
   b. REM
   c. LOL

4. Koalas need a lot of sleep. About how much do they get each day?
   a. 22 hours
   b. 12 hours
   c. 2 hours

5. What is it called when a person can't sleep?
   a. Insomnia
   b. Outsomnia
   c. College

6. Humans are the only creatures who dream.
   a. True
   b. False
   c. No one dreams.

7. What is the name of the mythical creature that visits during sleep?
   a. Mr. Sandy
   b. Sandman
   c. Sleepy the Dwarf

8. Sea otters occasionally link paws while snoozing to avoid drifting apart.
   a. True
   b. False
   c. Only sea otter babies do this.

9. How many hours a day do elephants sleep on average?
   a. 20 hours
   b. 9 hours
   c. 2 hours

10. You cannot sneeze during the deepest stages of sleep.
    a. True
    b. False
    c. It depends on what you ate that day.

chameleon course

Come along with these chameleons! Use the chameleon symbols below to figure out the right path through the grid.

Move 1 space

RIGHT

Move 1 space

DOWN

UP

Move 1 space

Move 1 space

LEFT

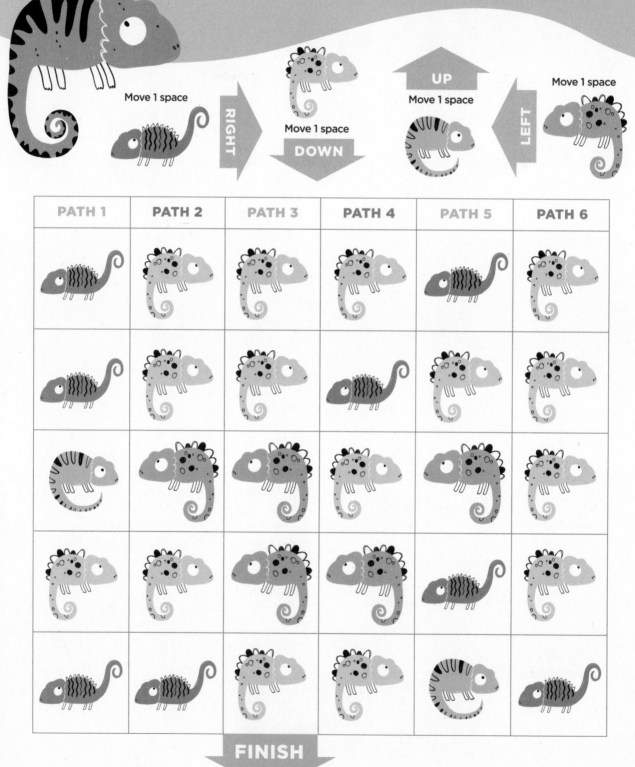

PATH 1	PATH 2	PATH 3	PATH 4	PATH 5	PATH 6

FINISH

curling chaos

Study this silly scene for two minutes. Then cover up everything except the green section below and try to answer the questions.

Test your memory!

1. Can you name at least one of the teams listed on the scorebaord?
2. What type drink is the cat selling at the judges' table?
3. What is the whale in the stands snacking on?
4. What is the curling stone knocking over in the middle lane?
5. Can you remember the colors of the canoe holding the two bears?

answers

BRAIN BREAKS

pages 2-3

TEST YOUR EYESIGHT: It's a chameleon.
BE LOGICAL: Nine cows are in the barn.
NOTICE THE DETAILS:

Wheels Light bulbs Hand shape	Wheels Button panels	Wheels Body color Windups
Noses Light bulbs	Noses Button panels Hand shape Windups	Noses Body color
Type of legs Windups Light bulbs	Type of legs Button panels	Type of legs Body color Hand shape

STRETCH YOUR MATH SKILLS: Here are our answers. You may have found others.
$(2 - 2) \times 2 \times 2 \times 2 = 0$
$(2 + 2 + 2) \div 2 - 2 = 1$
$2 \times 2 - 2 + 2 - 2 = 2$
$2 \div 2 + 2 + 2 - 2 = 3$
$(2 + 2) \times 2 - 2 - 2 = 4$
$(2 + 2 + 2) \div 2 + 2 = 5$
DO A WORD WORKOUT: Orange, floor, orca, organ, motor, author.

LET'S SHIFT GEARS

page 4

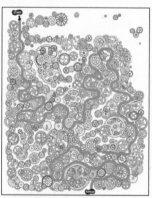

TULIP TIME page 5

The impostor is a teacup.

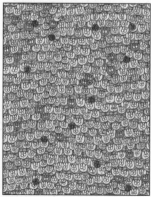

DEEP-SEA DINER

pages 6-7

BALLOON ANIMAL SUDOKU page 8

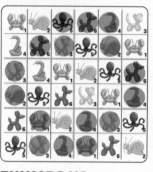

THUMBS UP page 9

DO THE ROBOT!

pages 10-11

PUZZLING PUPS page 12

WIGGLES: THREE YEARS OLD, NOAH, "COME"
ROCKET: TWO YEARS OLD, JAMIE, "SIT"
PAWLA: FOUR YEARS OLD, AMANDA, "HEEL"
60-SECOND STUMPER: What do you call a dog that designs doghouses? A BARK–ITECT.

CHECK IT OUT page 13

1. G **2.** H **3.** E **4.** C **5.** I **6.** B **7.** J **8.** D
9. A **10.** F

WHERE'S THE CAT?

pages 14-15

TRIVIA ANSWER: CATS CAN'T TASTE SWEETNESS.

LOTS OF LAUNDRY

pages 16-17

LOUNGING LLAMAS

page 18

BEACH DAY

page 19

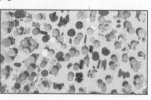

SWEET TREAT PATTERNS page 20

SNOWY VILLAGE

page 21

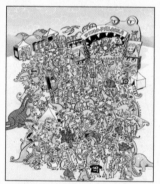

DINO MUSIC FEST

page 22

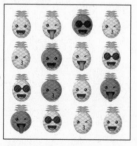

CREEPY CRAWLY QUIZZY page 23

1. T **2.** F **3.** F **4.** F **5.** T **6.** F **7.** T **8.** T **9.** F
10. T **11.** T **12.** T

BRAIN BREAKS

pages 24-25

BE LOGICAL:

TEST YOUR EYESIGHT: It's a sponge.
DO A WORD WORKOUT: Trout, shout, spout, snout, dugout.

STRETCH YOUR MATH SKILLS:

CRYSTAL CLEAR

pages 26–27

60-Second Stumper: Zetrocite

ESCAPE THE CAVE

pages 28–29

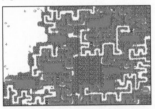

WHAT'S A ZIPZOP?

page 30

Zipzops have 2 square eyes, 4 circles on their bodies, and 3 spoon-shaped knobs.

SEASHELL SHADOW MATCH page 31

DOUGH-LICIOUS DELIGHTS pages 32–33

We found these rhymes. You may have found others.
A. THROW **B.** CROW **C.** YO-YO **D.** BLOW
E. HOE **F.** SEW **G.** GLOW **H.** SNOW **I.** TOW

SEA STAR SEARCH

page 34

The impostor is an octopus.

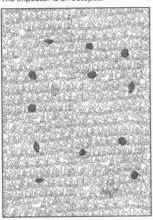

SLOTH RACE page 35

LOCK MESS page 36

1. E **2.** B **3.** L **4.** G **5.** F **6.** K **7.** C **8.** H **9.** J
10. D **11.** I **12.** A
60-SECOND STUMPER: A piano.

MONSTER SUDOKU

page 37

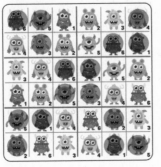

SNOW DAY! pages 38–39

ICE-CREAM CHALLENGE page 40

1. VANILLA **2.** CHOCOLATE **3.** COOKIES AND CREAM **4.** MINT CHOCOLATE CHIP
5. CHOCOLATE CHIP COOKIE DOUGH
6. BUTTER PECAN **7.** COOKIE DOUGH
8. STRAWBERRY **9.** MOOSE TRACKS
10. NEAPOLITAN
60-SECOND STUMPER: C

HAVE A SEAT page 41

1. Frank **2.** Iris **3.** Aiden **4.** Grace
5. Jada **6.** Eric **7.** Haley **8.** Carlos
9. Dave **10.** Lily **11.** Brian **12.** Katie

PIGEON PAIRS pages 42–43

TRAFFIC CHECK page 44

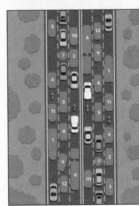

DOG DAYS page 45

1. E **2.** H **3.** C **4.** B **5.** D **6.** G **7.** A **8.** F

BRAIN BREAKS

pages 46–47
BE LOGICAL: You pour the juice from the second glass into the fifth glass.
DO A WORD WORKOUT:
1. CATNAP/NAPKIN
2. LIGHTHOUSE/HOUSEKEEPER
3. HORSEBACK/BACKYARD
4. SLEEPOVER/OVERBOARD
5. SNOWMAN/MANKIND
6. STARFISH/FISHNET
STRETCH YOUR MATH SKILLS: A. 10, 8
B. 14, 6 **C.** 21, 6
TEST YOUR EYESIGHT: It's an ocean wave.

answers

WELCOME TO SILLYVILLE page 48

BONUS: WHY IS IT BETTER TO EAT DOUGHNUTS IN THE RAIN?
BECAUSE YOU GET MORE SPRINKLES.

TIC TAC CAKE page 49

BLUE PLATE FLOWERS TWO TIERS	FLOWERS CHECKERED	FLOWERS HOT PINK COLOR TEAL COLOR
BLUE PLATE ARCHES	ARCHES TWO TIERS TEAL COLOR CHECKERED	HOT PINK COLOR ARCHES
BLUE PLATE HEARTS TEAL COLOR	CHECKERED HEARTS	HOT PINK COLOR TWO TIERS HEARTS

RINK THINK page 50

HUGO: Arrived at 1:30, hot cocoa
NORA: Arrived at 1:45, soft pretzel
GUNNAR: Arrived at 1:15, hot dog
URSULA: Arrived at 1:00, ice cream

WALL ART page 51

answers

SWEET INVENTION
page 52

SUMS AND SLICES
page 53

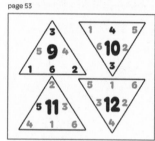

GO TEAM! pages 54-55

UNDER THE MICROSCOPE page 56

A GAGGLE OF GIRAFFES page 57
The impostor is a camel.

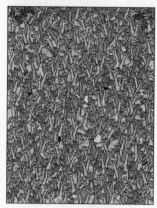

WACKY WORDS page 58
1. G 2. D 3. A 4. E 5. B 6. I 7. F 8. H
9. C 10. J

CACTUS PATTERNS
page 59

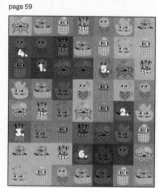

ONE ODD AIRPORT
page 60

1. Takeoff airport
2. Fish
3. A pterodactyl
4. A cactus
5. A surfboard

TRICKY STACKS page 61
1. 15 2. 13 3. 18 4. 15 5. 12 6. 16

SOCKS GALORE! page 62

STICK BUG ART CLASS page 63

GIMME SPACE! page 64
1. A 2. A 3. B 4. A 5. A 6. B 7. A 8. C
9. B 10. B

BIKE RACE page 65

ARCTIC ANIMAL SEARCH page 66

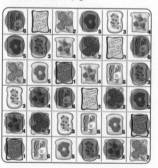

TASTY TOAST SUDOKU page 67

BRAIN BREAKS
pages 68-69
FIND THE PATTERN: 1. E 2. J 3. I 4. H 5. G
6. A 7. C 8. B 9. F 10. D
BE LOGICAL: Neither. Both weigh a pound.
STRETCH YOUR MATH SKILLS: 3 of each.
TEST YOUR EYESIGHT: It's a red onion.
DO A WORD WORKOUT: 1. He added
2. to every 3. Should Erin 4. beach in
5. both umbrellas 6. tank leaked

ALPINE ADVENTURES pages 70-71

CANDY COUNTER
page 72

🍬 = 5¢	**1.** $5 + 5 + 5 + 5 + 5 = 25$
🍭 = 9¢	**2.** $9 + 9 = 9 + 9$
🍬 = 7¢	**3.** $7 - 7 + 7 + 7 = 14$
🍫 = 6¢	**4.** $18 - 6 - 6 = 6$
🍫 = 8¢	**5.** $8 + 8 + 8 + 8 = 24 + 8$
🍬 = 2¢	**6.** $14 - 2 - 2 - 2 = 6$
🍭 = 4¢	**7.** $4 + 4 + 6 - 2 = 4 + 8$
❤ = 3¢	**8.** $3 + 3 + 3 = 12 - 3$

MIDDLE AGES MIX-UP page 73

BBQ CROSSWORD
pages 74-75

D R A B ■ S A D ■ B R O
O I L Y ■ A L E ■ S L A P
C O L E S L A W ■ Q U I T
■ ■ ■ B U S ■ ■ B U R N
B A B Y B A C K R I B S ■
A R I E S ■ H E R D ■ ■ ■
R E D ■ B U Y ■ D I M
■ ■ P A I R ■ C R E D O
C O R N O N T H E C O B
H U E Y ■ R I D ■ ■ ■
H I T S ■ I C E C R E A M
O N E S ■ T O N ■ E R I E
T A R ■ S O D ■ W A R N

FROG CODE page 76
FOUR FAST FROGS FLYING
PAST FAST.

SHADOW MATCH
page 77

IT'S A WRAP
page 84

AMBER: GREEN GIFT, BLUE BOW
BILLY: BLUE GIFT, YELLOW BOW
CHAD: RED GIFT, GREEN BOW
DAPHNE: YELLOW GIFT, RED BOW

TREE TRAILS

page 85

BONUS: What is the biggest ant in the world? ELEPHANT.

AUSSIE ANIMALS
pages 86–87

OWL SUDOKU page 92

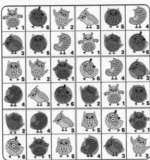

CATCH YOUR FLIGHT page 93
The green path will get you to your gate in 37 minutes, before your flight leaves.

HIDE-AND-SEEK page 94

BUTTON SET page 95

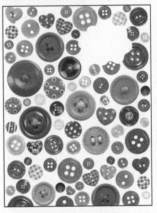

answers

ON YOUR LEFT! page 99

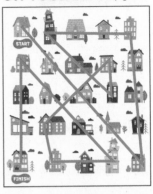

ALL THE AVOCADOS
page 100
The impostor is a green pepper.

SNACK PATH page 78

PENGUINS WITH PUCKS page 79

BEE CAREFUL page 80
1. A 2. G 3. I 4. F 5. C 6. J 7. B 8. E
9. D 10. H

READY, SET, GO! page 81
A tire by a dryer, a kart by a heart, a traffic cone by a phone, a steering wheel by a banana peel, trees by skis, a hat by a cat, a two by a shoe, a flower by a shower, and a flag by a bag.
   We found these things that rhyme with go. (You may have found others.) Buffalo, dough, crow, snow, hoe, bow, arrow, and banjo.

SUPER-DUPER PANCAKE MAKER
pages 82–83

FARM FRENZY page 88
1. Corn 2. "Mooooo" 3. A slice of cake
4. A rocking chair 5. Basketball

SNACK ATTACK PATTERNS page 89

BRAIN BREAKS
pages 90–91
BE LOGICAL:

DO A WORD WORKOUT: Funny bunny, mouse house, soggy doggy, wordy birdy, wee bee, wary canary.
GUESSTIMATE: There are 55 fish in the group.
TEST YOUR EYESIGHT: It's lava.
STRETCH YOUR MATH SKILLS: A = 10; B = 2.

ADOPTION DAY!
pages 96–97

SPORTY SEARCH
page 98

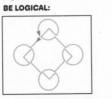

AT THE MOVIES
pages 102–103

answers

RAIN OR SHINE

pages 104–105

BLOCKS ROCK! page 106

1. A 2. H 3. F 4. D 5. G 6. C 7. E 8. I
9. J 10. B

ESCAPE-ROOM FUN

page 107

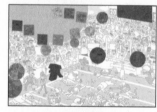

STADIUM SNAPSHOTS

pages 108–109

BRAIN BREAKS

pages 110–111

BE LOGICAL: 1. 6:16 **2.** 12:01 **3.** 5:23
4. 9:30
STRETCH YOUR MATH SKILLS:
The highest total is 30.

TEST YOUR EYESIGHT: It's an escalator.
DO A WORD WORKOUT: Meow, game, home, camel, summer, America.

TREE SHADOW MATCH pages 112–113

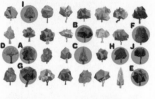

SEA CAT CIRCUIT

page 114

SPRINKLE SEARCH

page 115

HIDING IN THE GRASS

page 116

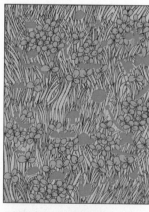

PHOTO FINISH

page 117

ANNIE: FAMILY, 2ND
GEORGE: HOUSE, HONORABLE MENTION
ROBERT: HORSE, 3RD
SOPHIE: LANDSCAPE, 1ST

BY THE NUMBERS

page 118

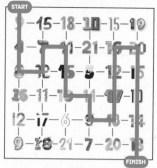

SLURPING SNAKES

page 119

OCEAN QUIZ

page 120

1. False 2. True 3. True 4. False 5. True
6. True 7. True 8. False 9. True 10. False
11. True 12. True 13. False 14. True
15. False

SUPERMARKET SEARCH page 121

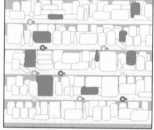

SANDY STUMPER

page 122

beach ball sunglasses green-and-white towel	beach ball surfboard	beach ball snorkel gear shovel and pail
flip-flops sunglasses	flip-flops surfboard green-and-white towel shovel and pail	flip-flops snorkel gear
crab shovel and pail sunglasses	crab surfboard	crab snorkel gear green-and-white towel

60-SECOND STUMPER: 1. swimsuit
2. towel **3.** surfboard **4.** goggles
5. flip-flops **6.** book

SPORTS SPEAK

page 123

1. D 2. A 3. H. 4. E 5. B. 6. F. 7. C. 8. I.
9. J. 10. G.

PRIMATE HEAD-SCRATCHER pages 124–125

WHEN DO GORILLAS PLAY BASEBALL?
IN APE-RIL.

COOKIE CONUNDRUM page 126

1. MACAROON 2. LEMON BAR 3. SUGAR
4. FORTUNE 5. GINGERSNAP
6. SHORTBREAD 7. OATMEAL RAISIN
8. PEANUT BUTTER 9. CHOCOLATE CHIP
10. SNICKERDOODLE
BONUS: What did the gingerbread man use to trim his fingernails?
A COOKIE CUTTER.

ZANY DINER page 127

1. MOONBEAM DINER 2. A BURGER AND
FRIES 3. OIL 4. RED 5. A MOUSE

SNEAKER SEEKERS

pages 128–129

BRAIN BREAKS

pages 130–131

BE LOGICAL: Today is Alex's birthday.
Statements 2 and 3 are the only two statements that can be false at the same time. That means only statement 1 can be true.
DO A WORD WORKOUT: 1. Things that flip. **2.** Things with eyes. **3.** Things with tails. **4.** Things that pop. **5.** Things with horns.
TEST YOUR EYESIGHT: They're bird feathers.
STRETCH YOUR MATH SKILLS: Move the 9 from column C and add it to column A.

answers

COLORFUL CHAOS
page 132

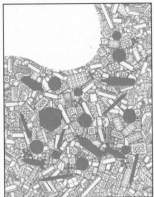

SPACING OUT
page 138

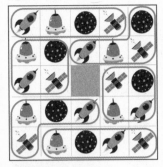

CLUSTER OF CONES
page 139

The impostor is a cupcake.

MUSHROOM SUDOKU
page 133

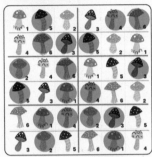

JELLY JAMBOREE
page 143

BATTER UP
pages 144–145

60-SECOND STUMPER
B. AROUND 90 MPH

SKATEBOARD LOGIC
page 146

1. DILLON: PURPLE, $80 2. REESE: BLUE, $50 3. ANDREW: ORANGE, $70 4. ANNA: YELLOW, $60

NICE ICE
page 147

ANIMAL ARCADE
pages 134–135

FEATHERY FRACTIONS
page 140

1. TWEET-MENT.
2. THE CON-DUCK-TOR.
3. A SWALLOW.

PRAIRIE DOG HOTEL
page 141

LLAMA PAJAMA PARTY
pages 148–149

BONUS
The rhyming things in this picture are:
A poodle with a noodle
A bat with a hat
A goat in a coat
A bug on a mug
A king on a swing
A pig in a wig
A heart on a tart

WHICH WAY IS UP?
page 136

FISH FEST
page 137

BUTTERFLY BONANZA
page 142

1. G. 2. F. 3. J. 4. D. 5. E. 6. B. 7. I. 8. H. 9. A. 10. C.

IT'S CAMPY
pages 150–151

BONUS: WHAT DO OCTOPUSES TAKE ON CAMPING TRIPS? TENT-ACLES.

BRAIN BREAKS
pages 152–153

BE LOGICAL: CHEF NOODLE ONLY COOKS FOODS WITH DOUBLE LETTERS IN THEIR NAMES.

STRETCH YOUR MATH SKILLS:
A. $9 + 5 = 14$ B. $4 \times 3 = 12$ C. $2 + 8 = 10$ D. $1 + 7 = 8$ E. $0 + 6 = 6$

TEST YOUR EYESIGHT:
IT'S HOT CHOCOLATE.

DO A WORD WORKOUT: We found these. You may have found others.
1. SHOP, STORE 2. FEAR, FRIGHT, 3. SPOT, SPECK, 4. DART, DASH, 5. PLATE, PLATTER, 6. BRING, BEAR 7. GRIP, GRASP 8. SHAVE, SHEAR

GIZMO AND GERTIE'S BOT-TACULAR DAY
pages 154–155

GIZMO'S DAY: 1. G 2. E 3. B 4. I 5. A 6. D 7. C 8. F 9. H

GERTIE'S DAY: 1. C 2. I 3. H 4. B 5. F 6. A 7. E 8. D 9. G

BONUS: GIZMO AND GERTIE ALMOST CROSS PATHS AT 3:00.

SIT. STAY. SNACK!
pages 156–157

BONUS: TASTY LETTERS
1. Rice
2. Bread
3. Pear
4. Olive
5. Chips
6. Noodles
7. Peach
8. Prune

answers

THE CASE OF THE CREEPY CRAWLY

page 158

RED PANDA EXTRAVAGANZA

page 159

THAT'S A LOTTA AXOLOTLS! page 160

BONUS: 60-SECOND STUMPER
1. ATOLL
2. TOOL
3. TALL
4. LOT

LEAFY LABYRINTH

page 161

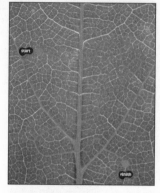

GET CRAFTY

pages 162–163

WHAT'S BLUE AND SMELLS LIKE GREEN PAINT? BLUE PAINT

FLYING SQUIRRELS

page 164

CLASSIC DUOS

page 165

PEANUT BUTTER AND JELLY, MILK AND COOKIES, HAMMER AND NAIL, LOCK AND KEY, SPAGHETTI AND MEATBALLS, MACARONI AND CHEESE, APPLES AND ORANGES, BOW AND ARROW, DOGS AND CATS, THUNDER AND LIGHTNING SHAMPOO AND CONDITIONER, NEEDLE AND THREAD.

NIGHT AND DAY

page 166

SLEEP QUIZZZ

page 167

1. A 2. A 3. B 4. A 5. A 6. B 7. B 8. A
9. C 10. A

CHAMELEON COURSE

page 168

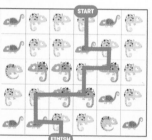

CURLING CHAOS

page 169

1. MOOSE, ELEPHANTS, OR BEARS
2. LEMONADE
3. POPCORN
4. BOWLING PINS
5. ORANGE AND YELLOW

FRONT COVER

BACK COVER

COVER ART BY SHAW NIELSEN

PHOTO AND ILLUSTRATION CREDITS: Tim Alexander (66); Paula Becker (65); Aaron Blecha (154–155); Paula Bossio (96–97); Jim Bradshaw (158); Annika Brandow (16–17, 57, 89, 148–149); Jamie Coe (101); Daryll Collins (38–39, 144–145); Catherine Copeland (26–27); Lee Cosgrove (119); Amanda Cotan (136); Victor Davila (90); Luke Flowers (70–71); Travis Foster (5, 34, 41, 68, 116, 139); Getty Images (2, 8, 9, 12, 13, 14–15, 20, 23, 24, 25, 26–27, 31, 37, 40, 42–43, 45, 46, 47, 49, 50, 53, 54–55, 56, 59, 62, 64, 67, 68, 69, 72, 74–75, 76, 80, 84, 86–87, 91, 92, 95, 99, 102–103, 104–105, 106, 110, 111, 112–113, 114, 115, 117, 118, 120, 124–125, 130, 131, 133, 137, 138, 140, 142, 146, 150–151, 152, 153, 156–157, 160, 161, 162–163, 167, 168); Bill Golliher (156–157); Jennifer Harney (51, 107, 147); Esther Hernando (94); Don Hill (19); Alexander Jansson (166); Jango Jim/ Dimitri (30); Kelly Kennedy (60, 165, 169); Annette Kiesow (90); Greg Kletsel (108–109, 143); Lauren Ko (49); Ken Krug (161); Gary LaCoste (6–7, 35, 134–135, 164); Pat Lewis (81); Matt Lyon (21, 78, 141); Jennifer Maravillas-Bell (77); Bill McConkey (132); Valentina Mendicino (18); Victor Medina (44); Emiliano Migliardo (123); Meredith Miotke (93); Shaw Nielsen (32–33, 36, 73, 110, 121, 122); Chris Piascik (58); Rich Powell (82–83, 115); Merrill Rainey (46–47); Alex Ram (98); Andy Romanchik (85); Joel Santana (61); Shutterstock (3, 126, 128–129); Erica Sirotich (100); Jack Viant (52); Jaka Vukotič (4, 28–29); Brian Michael Weaver (63, 79); Tim Wesson (159); Dave Whamond (22, 48, 88, 127); Brian White (10–11); Kevin Zimmer (20)

For information about permission to reprint selections from this book, please contact permissions@highlights.com.

Published by Highlights Press
815 Church Street
Honesdale, Pennsylvania 18431
ISBN: 978-1-63962-250-4
Manufactured in
Jefferson City, MO, USA
Mfg. 06/2024

First edition
Visit our website at Highlights.com.
10 9 8 7 6 5 4 3 2 1

Produced by WonderLab Group
Design: Nicole Lazarus
Photo Editor: Annette Kiesow